# The Ethics of Euthanasia

## ISSUES

## Volume 102

Editor

Craig Donnellan

*Independence*

**Educational Publishers**
Cambridge

First published by Independence
PO Box 295
Cambridge CB1 3XP
England

**British Library Cataloguing in Publication Data**
The Ethics of Euthanasia  – (Issues Series)
I. Donnellan, Craig II. Series
179.7

ISBN 1 86168 316 2

**Printed in Great Britain**
MWL Print Group Ltd

**Typeset by**
Claire Boyd

**Cover**
The illustration on the front cover is by
Pumpkin House.

# CONTENTS

# Introduction

*The Ethics of Euthanasia* is the hundred and second volume in the **Issues** series. The aim of this series is to offer up-to-date information about important issues in our world.

*The Ethics of Euthanasia* looks at the moral and medical dilemma of euthanasia, and living wills.

The information comes from a wide variety of sources and includes:
Government reports and statistics
Newspaper reports and features
Magazine articles and surveys
Web site material
Literature from lobby groups
and charitable organisations.

It is hoped that, as you read about the many aspects of the issues explored in this book, you will critically evaluate the information presented. It is important that you decide whether you are being presented with facts or opinions. Does the writer give a biased or an unbiased report? If an opinion is being expressed, do you agree with the writer?

*The Ethics of Euthanasia* offers a useful starting-point for those who need convenient access to information about the many issues involved. However, it is only a starting-point. At the back of the book is a list of organisations which you may want to contact for further information.

\*\*\*\*\*

# A non-religious perspective on euthanasia

### Some definitions

- Euthanasia originally meant 'a gentle and easy death', and is now used to mean 'the act of inducing an easy death', usually referring to acts which terminate or shorten life painlessly in order to end suffering where there is no prospect of recovery.
- Voluntary euthanasia, sometimes called 'assisted suicide', is used in cases where the sufferer has made it clear that s/he wishes to die and has requested help to bring this about.
- Involuntary euthanasia occurs when no consent or wish to die is expressed by the sufferer. One can, and perhaps should, further distinguish between cases where patients cannot express a wish to die (patients in comas, infants, cases of extreme senile dementia), sometimes called non-voluntary euthanasia, and those where they can but don't, called involuntary.
- Active, or direct, euthanasia involves specific actions (e.g. lethal drugs or injections) intended to bring about death. This is illegal in Great Britain.
- Passive euthanasia is the practice, widely carried out and generally judged to be legal, where patients are allowed to die, by withdrawing treatment and/or nourishment.
- Indirect euthanasia (sometimes referred to as 'the double effect') is the practice of providing treatment, normally pain relief, which has the side-effect of hastening death. This is also widely practised and generally considered legal if killing was not the intention.

### The problem

Arguments about euthanasia often hinge on the 'right to life' and the

'right to die'. The first is a widely accepted basic human right and moral value, based on the fact that people generally want to live. But what should we do when seriously ill people no longer want to live? Do they have a right to die? Sufferers sometimes wish to commit suicide but do not have the physical strength or the means to do it painlessly.

Like many problems of medical ethics, this has become more pressing recently. A century ago most people died quite quickly (and probably painfully) if they had serious injuries or illnesses. Nowadays they can be treated, sometimes cured, and often kept alive almost indefinitely. Codes of conduct formulated centuries ago, for example those found in sacred texts, or the Hippocratic oath, cannot necessarily help us with twenty-first-century problems of medical ethics.

### The humanist view

Humanists are non-religious people who live by moral principles based on reason and respect for others, not obedience to dogmatic rules. They promote happiness and fulfilment in this life because they believe it is the only one we have. Humanist concern for quality of life and respect for personal autonomy leads to the view that in many circumstances voluntary euthanasia is the morally right course. People should have the right to choose a painless and dignified end, either at the time or beforehand, perhaps in a 'living will'. The right circumstances might include: extreme pain and suffering; helplessness and loss of personal dignity; permanent loss of those things which have made life worth living for this individual. To postpone the inevitable with no intervening benefit is not a moral act. Individuals should be allowed to decide on such personal matters for themselves. So humanists generally support voluntary euthanasia, whilst upholding the need for safeguards to prevent involuntary euthanasia.

There is no rational moral distinction between allowing someone to die and actively assisting them to die in these circumstances: the intention and the outcome (the death of the patient) are the same in both cases, but the more active means is probably the more compassionate one. The BHA supports attempts to reform the current law on voluntary euthanasia.

## Safeguards

If someone in possession of full information and sound judgement decides that her continued life has no value, her wishes should be respected. Of course there should be safeguards: counselling; the prevention of pressure on patients; clear witnessed instructions from the patient; the involvement of several doctors; no reasonable hope of recovery.

## Some other arguments

The 'slippery slope' or 'thin end of the wedge' argument says that if you permit voluntary euthanasia, involuntary euthanasia will follow. Hitler's programme of euthanasia is often cited – but this was clearly involuntary euthanasia carried out by a murderous dictator who did not begin by offering voluntary euthanasia to terminally ill hospital patients who had requested it; no 'slippery slope' was involved. The boundary between voluntary and involuntary euthanasia is a very distinct one and not difficult to maintain.

People often argue that it is not for doctors 'to play God' and that it's for God to decide when people die. But it could be said that all medical interventions are 'playing God' (even your childhood vaccinations may have kept you alive longer than 'God' planned) so we have to decide for ourselves how we use medical powers. Arguments which invoke God are unconvincing to those who do not believe in gods, and laws should not be based on claims which rely on religious faith.

Religious people also often use phrases like 'the sanctity of life' to justify the view that life has intrinsic value and must not be destroyed. Humanists, too, see a special value in human life, but think that if an individual has decided on rational grounds that his life has lost its meaning and value, that evaluation should be respected.

Some religious people maintain that there is a moral distinction between acts which cause death (active euthanasia) and omissions which cause death (passive euthanasia), only the second being morally permissible. Many humanists think they've got it the wrong way round, because the first is quicker and thus kinder for everyone involved, though both are probably painless for the patient.

Many of the medical profession and politicians have also accepted this traditional distinction. It might be easier for doctors to withdraw or withhold treatment than it would be for them to administer a lethal drug – but this does not necessarily make it right. It would be wrong to force doctors and nurses to do things that they consider morally wrong, but patients wishing assistance in dying should be allowed to seek a doctor who will help them.

If one believes that suicide is wrong (and it can cause great pain to those left behind), then assisted suicide, seemingly, must be wrong too. But the death of a terminally ill and suffering patient would probably be a merciful release for everyone involved and so is very different in its effects from other suicides.

■ The above information is from the British Humanist Association's website which can be found at www.humanism.org.uk

*© British Humanist Association*
*December 2004*

# *So you think you know about euthanasia?*

### By Diana E. Forrest

*False belief:*
'Quality of life' is a clear concept that will make euthanasia decisions easy.

*Truth:*
'Quality of life' is worryingly vague. Does it mean that poor people will be more likely to undergo euthanasia than rich people? Does it mean that disabled people are more likely to undergo it than non-disabled people?

*False belief:*
Money won't come into euthanasia decisions.

*Truth:*
At a conference of the General Medical Council held in July 2001, Dame Elizabeth Butler-Sloss said that hospitals may need to consider the issue of resources.

*False belief:*
Euthanasia is just a matter of withholding burdensome medical treatment.

*Truth:*
Food and water have been redefined as medical treatment.

*False belief:*
Euthanasia works well in the Netherlands and people there are happy about it.

*Truth:*
The Dutch senate got 60,000 letters opposing euthanasia. It has been used on people who were depressed but not physically ill.

■ The above information is from Alert's website which can be found at www.donoharm.org.uk/alert

*© Alert*

# Euthanasia and assisted suicide

## Frequently asked questions

By Rita L. Marker
and Kathi Hamlon

One of the most important public policy debates today surrounds the issues of euthanasia and assisted suicide. The outcome of that debate will profoundly affect family relationships, interaction between doctors and patients, and concepts of basic ethical behaviour. With so much at stake, more is needed than a duel of one-liners, slogans and sound bites.

The following answers to frequently asked questions are designed as starting points for considering the issues.

### Where are euthanasia and assisted suicide legal?

Oregon, the Netherlands and Belgium are the only jurisdictions in the world where laws specifically permit euthanasia or assisted suicide. Oregon permits assisted suicide.[1] The Netherlands and Belgium permit both euthanasia and assisted suicide.[2]

In 1995 Australia's Northern Territory approved a euthanasia bill.[3] It went into effect in 1996 but was overturned by the Australian Parliament in 1997. Also, in 1997, Colombia's Supreme Court ruled that penalties for mercy killing should be removed.[4] However the ruling does not go into effect until guidelines, still to be drafted, are approved by the Colombian Congress.

### What is the difference between euthanasia and assisted suicide?

One way to distinguish them is to look at the last act – the act without which death would not occur.

Using this distinction, if a third party performs the last act that intentionally causes a patient's death, euthanasia has occurred. For example, giving a patient a lethal injection or putting a plastic bag over her head to suffocate her would be considered euthanasia.

On the other hand, if the person who dies performs the last act, assisted suicide has taken place. Thus it would be assisted suicide if a person swallows an overdose of drugs that has been provided by a doctor for the purpose of causing death. It would also be assisted suicide if a patient pushes a switch to trigger a fatal injection after the doctor has inserted an intravenous needle into the patient's vein.

### Doesn't modern technology keep people alive who would have died in the past?

Modern medicine has definitely lengthened life spans. A century ago, high blood pressure, pneumonia, appendicitis, and diabetes likely meant death, often accompanied by excruciating pain. Women had shorter life expectancies than men since many died in childbirth. Antibiotics, immunisations, modern surgery and many of today's routine therapies or medications were unknown then.

### Should people be forced to stay alive?

No. A lot of people think that euthanasia or assisted suicide is needed so patients won't be forced to remain alive by being 'hooked up' to machines. But the law already permits patients or their surrogates to withhold or withdraw unwanted medical treatment even if that increases the likelihood that the patient will die. Thus, no one needs to be hooked up to machines against their will.

Neither the law nor medical ethics requires that 'everything be done' to keep a person alive. Insistence, against the patient's wishes, that death be postponed by every means available is contrary to law and practice. It is also cruel and inhumane.

There comes a time when continued attempts to cure are not compassionate, wise, or medically sound. That's when hospice, including in-home hospice care, can

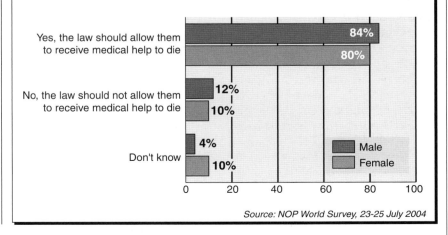

**The law and euthanasia**

*Do you think that a person who is suffering unbearably from a terminal illness should be allowed by law to receive medical help to die, if this is what they want? Or should the law not allow them to receive this medical help to die?*

- Yes, the law should allow them to receive medical help to die: 84% / 80%
- No, the law should not allow them to receive medical help to die: 12% / 10%
- Don't know: 4% / 10%

Male
Female

Source: NOP World Survey, 23-25 July 2004

be of great help. That is the time when all efforts should be directed to making the patient's remaining time comfortable. Then, all interventions should be directed to alleviating pain and other symptoms as well as to the provision of emotional and spiritual support for both the patient and the patient's loved ones.

### But shouldn't people have the right to commit suicide?

People do have the power to commit suicide. Worldwide, about a million people commit suicide annually.[5] Suicide and attempted suicide are not criminalised. Each and every year, in the United States alone, there are 1.5 times as many suicides as there are homicides.[6] And suicide is one of the ten most common causes of death in Great Britain.[7]

Suicide is an all too common tragic, individual act. Indeed, the Surgeon General of the United States is currently campaigning to reduce the rate of suicide.[8]

Euthanasia and assisted suicide are not private acts. Rather, they involve one person facilitating the death of another. This is a matter of very public concern since it can lead to tremendous abuse, exploitation and erosion of care for the most vulnerable people among us.

Euthanasia and assisted suicide are not about giving rights to the person who dies but, instead, they are about changing public policy so that doctors or others can directly and intentionally end or participate in ending another person's life. Euthanasia and assisted suicide are not about the right to die. They are about the right to kill.

### Isn't 'kill' too strong a word for euthanasia and assisted suicide?

No. The word 'kill' means 'to cause the death of'.[9]

In 1989, a group of physicians published a report in the *New England Journal of Medicine* in which they concluded that it would be morally acceptable for doctors to give patients suicide information and a prescription for deadly drugs so they can kill themselves.[10] Dr Ronald Cranford, one of the authors of the report, publicly acknowledged that this was 'the same as killing the patient'.[11]

While changes in laws have transformed euthanasia and assisted suicide from crimes into 'medical treatments' in Oregon and the Netherlands, the reality has not changed – patients are being killed.

Proponents of euthanasia and assisted suicide often use euphemisms like 'deliverance', 'death with dignity', 'aid-in-dying' and 'gentle landing'. If a proposed change in public policy has to be promoted with euphemisms, this may be due to the fact that the use of accurate, descriptive language would make its chilling reality too obvious.

### Certainly people wouldn't be forced into euthanasia or assisted suicide, would they?

Oregon's assisted suicide law does not allow anyone to 'coerce' or use 'undue influence' to obtain a request for assisted suicide.[12] However, there is absolutely nothing in the Oregon law to prevent HMOs, managed care companies, doctors or anyone else from suggesting, encouraging, offering, or bringing up assisted suicide with a patient who has not asked about it.

Emotional, financial and psychological pressures could become overpowering for depressed or dependent people. If the choice of euthanasia or assisted suicide is considered as good as a decision to receive care, some people will feel guilty for not choosing death.

The concern about 'being a burden' could serve as a powerful force that could influence the decision. The third annual report on deaths under the Oregon assisted suicide law illustrates this. In 63% of the deaths reported, fear of being a burden was expressed as a reason for requesting assisted suicide.[13]

Even the smallest gesture could create a gentle nudge into the grave. Such was evidenced in greeting cards sold at a national conference of the Hemlock Society.

According to the conference programme, the cards were designed to be given to those who are terminally ill. One card in particular exemplified the core of the movement that would remove the last shred of hope remaining to a person faced with a life-threatening illness. It carried the message, 'I learned you'll be leaving us soon.'[14]

### Isn't euthanasia or assisted suicide sometimes the only way to relieve excruciating pain?

Quite the contrary. Euthanasia activists exploit the natural fear people have of suffering and dying. They often claim that, without euthanasia or assisted suicide, people will be forced to endure unbearable pain:

During a radio debate, T. Patrick Hill (who was then an official of Choice in Dying and currently serves on the board of directors of the New York Citizens' Committee on Health Care Decisions) stated that continuing to prohibit euthanasia would, in some circumstances, 'abandon the patient to a horrifying death'.[15]

Hill acknowledged that 'even under the best circumstances active euthanasia is indeed a troubling issue'. But he said, 'I do think there are very restricted circumstances where, in fact, it is the more humane thing to do rather than not to do. Because, not to do it would, as I say, be to abandon the patient to unbearable suffering, whether emotional suffering or physical suffering.'[16]

Such irresponsible claims fail to recognise that virtually all pain can be eliminated or that – in those rare cases where it can't be totally eliminated – it can be reduced significantly if proper treatment is provided.

It is a national and international scandal that so many people do not get adequate pain control. But killing is not the answer to that scandal. The solution is to mandate better education of health care professionals on these crucial issues, to expand access to health care, and to inform patients about their rights as consumers.

In 2001, the International Task Force published an important new book, *Power over Pain*, which is an incredibly valuable tool for people to use in obtaining the pain relief they need.

Everyone – whether a person with a life-threatening illness or a chronic condition – has the right to pain relief. With modern advances in pain control, no patient should ever be in excruciating pain. However most doctors have never had a course in pain management so they're unaware of what to do.

If a patient who is under a doctor's care is in excruciating pain, there's definitely a need to find a different doctor. But that doctor should be one who will control the pain, not one who will kill the patient.

There are board certified specialists in pain management who can not only help alleviate physical pain but who are also skilled in providing necessary support to deal with emotional suffering and depression that often accompany physical pain.

### Since suicide isn't against the law, why should it be illegal to help someone commit suicide?

Neither suicide nor attempted suicide is criminalised anywhere in the United States or in many other countries. This is not because of any 'right' to suicide. When penalties against attempted suicide were removed, legal scholars made it clear that this was not done for the purpose of permitting suicide. Instead it was intended to prevent suicide. Penalties were removed so people could seek help in dealing with the

---

*Everyone has the right to pain relief. With modern advances in pain control, no patient should ever be in excruciating pain*

---

problems they're facing without risk of being prosecuted if it were discovered that they had attempted suicide.

Just as current public policy does not grant a 'right' to be killed to a person who is suicidal because of a lost business, neither should it permit people to be killed because they are in despair over their physical or emotional condition. With legalised euthanasia or assisted suicide, condemned killers would have more rights to have their lives protected than would vulnerable people who could be pressured and exploited into what amounts to capital punishment for the 'crime' of being sick, old, disabled or dependent.

### Endnotes:

1  Oregon's 'Death with Dignity Act' (ORS 127.800-897) passed in November 1994 and went into effect in 1997.
2  Although both euthanasia and assisted suicide had been widely practised in the Netherlands, they remained technically illegal until passage of a bill for the 'Review of cases of termination of life on request and assistance with suicide' was approved in April 2001. Belgium's law was passed on May 16, 2002.
3  'Rights of the Terminally Ill Act,' Northern Territory of Australia (1996).
4  Republic of Colombia Constitutional Court, Sentence # c-239/97, Ref. Expedient # D-1490, May 20, 1997.
5  Medscape. Available at http://www.medscape.com/Medscape/psychiatry/clinicalMgmt/CM.v03/pnt-CM.v03.html, citing Jamison

K.R., *Night Falls Fast*, New York, NY: Alfred Knopf; 1999. Accessed 3/19/01.
6  In 1997, suicide took the lives of 30,535 people – 1.5 times as many as died from homicide. (http://www.cdc.gov/ncipc/factsheets/suifacts.htm) Center for Disease Control, accessed 4/6/01.
7  Alan J. Carson, Steven Best, et al., 'Suicidal ideation among outpatients at general neurology clinics: prospective study,' 320 *British Medical Journal* (May 13, 2000), p. 1311.
8  Anjetta McQueen, 'U.S. Launches Suicide Plan,' Associated Press, May 2, 2001.
9  *Webster's New World Dictionary of the American Language*, Second edition (1976).
10  Sidney H. Wanzer, M.D. et al., 'The Physician's Responsibility toward Hopelessly Ill Patients: A Second Look,' 320 *The New England Journal of Medicine* (March 30, 1989), p. 848.
11  *MacNeil/Lehrer NewsHour*, PBS, March 30, 1989.
12  Oregon 'Death with Dignity Act' [ORS 127.890 §4.02 (2)].
13  *Oregon Death with Dignity Act: Three Years of Legalized Physician-Assisted Suicide*, Oregon Health Division (February 21, 2001), Table 3.
14.  The greeting card was from 'Grief Songs' Greeting Cards. It was described on the programme and purchased at 'Reforming the Law: The 5th National Conference on Voluntary Euthanasia,' sponsored by the National Hemlock Society and the Metro Denver Hemlock Society, November 15 and 16, 1991 in Denver, Colorado. Card on file at International Task Force office.
15.  Transcript from audio tape of 'On Target,' WVON Radio (Chicago). Debate between Rita Marker and T. Patrick Hill, September 26, 1993.
16  Ibid.

■ The above information is from the International Task Force on Euthanasia and Assisted Suicide's website: www.internationaltaskforce.org

# Assisting the terminally ill

**A little sightseeing, a glass of schnapps, then a peaceful death in a suburban flat
In his first British interview, the founder of the Swiss suicide clinic explains how
he helps people take their lives**

*By Luke Harding in Zürich*

It is an anonymous fourth-floor flat, decorated with a sweeping view of the Swiss Alps, a fantasy landscape and an abstract painting. There is a bed and a couple of chairs. There is also a collection of walking sticks, left behind by patients who no longer need them. It is here, in a quiet suburb of Zürich, that at least 22 terminally ill Britons have spent their final moments. And if the public prosecutor fails to intervene, it is also where Mrs Z, the subject of a high court case this week, is likely to come next month to kill herself.

Mrs Z, who has an incurable brain disease, is one of more than 500 British patients who have registered with Dignitas, a non-profit organisation which assists the terminally ill to commit suicide.

A judge lifted a temporary injunction banning Mrs Z from making the trip and said it was now up to the police to decide what action to take under criminal law. Aiding a suicide is legal in Switzerland, but under the 1961 Suicide Act is punishable in Britain by up to 14 years in prison.

Since it was founded in 1998, Dignitas has helped patients from all over the world end their lives. Most of them have been suffering from incurable and painful conditions, like pancreatic or breast cancer or motor neurone disease.

Controversially, however, a small minority have been physically fit but suffering from severe and prolonged mental illnesses such as schizophrenia or depression.

In December 2004, Dignitas's Swiss founder Ludwig Minelli, a 72-year-old human rights lawyer and former journalist with *Der Spiegel* magazine, spoke to the *Guardian* in his first interview with a British newspaper. 'I believe that every person has the right to live or die. But I also believe that there is no obligation to carry on living,' Mr Minelli said, at his home in the village of Forch, just outside Zürich.

'There is no point in forcing elderly people to live in a situation they don't think is dignified. We should accept the demand of a human being to commit suicide. And we should make it an assisted suicide to avoid the risks that go with other attempts.'

> **'There is no point in forcing elderly people to live in a situation they don't think is dignified'**

Mr Minelli, a former legal adviser with the pro-euthanasia group Exit, said 80% of patients who approached his organisation did not commit suicide. But the fact that the possibility was there gave them enormous comfort, he said. About 1-2% died immediately afterwards anyway.

The procedure for those who wanted to go ahead was straightforward, Mr Minelli said. The first step was for Dignitas staff to 'green light' the member's application by establishing that they were capable of judgment and were not under pressure from family or other third

parties to end their lives. After that, patients would fly to Zürich with a close family member or friend, although some turned up alone. They would travel to Mr Minelli's house. Here, over cups of Japanese tea, and in a living room overflowing with books, Mr Minelli would ask the patient whether they were certain they wanted an assisted suicide. If the answer was yes, he called a doctor. The doctor would discuss the case with the patient and, if satisfied, prescribe a lethal 15ml dose of pentobarbital sodium, a barbiturate normally used by vets. Mr Minelli said the mood of most patients hours before their death was not gloomy or morbid but celebratory.

'They are happy. They are even joking. Sometimes they embrace me and say: "I'm delighted to be here." Of course in most cases the relatives are not so happy. Normally, two or three come. Once, 12 relatives came along and we drank a glass of wine together.'

Some terminally ill patients are even keen to do some last-minute sightseeing. 'I had an 80-year-old German lady suffering from motor neurone disease who said: "I want to get to know Zürich." She also wanted to drink a schnapps.

'I didn't have any schnapps so drove into the city and had lunch together in the Fifa restaurant, which has a panoramic view. We ate mushrooms and had two glasses of expensive wine. I suggested she had meringue for dessert – she had never tried it.

'She was so enthusiastic. She was very happy. And then she died.'

On the way to the apartment where the assisted suicides take place, Mr Minelli stops off at a chemist's to collect the lethal barbiturates. Upstairs, he says goodbye and leaves the patient in the hands of one of Dignitas's staff members, known in German as a *Freitodbegleiter*.

The staff member prepares an anti-emetic, to prevent the patient from vomiting. This takes half an hour to work. The patient is then given a glass of water containing the dissolved barbiturate. The staff member leaves.

Most crucially, the patient then has to drink the drug himself or herself – or flick a switch on a pump which injects the drug intravenously. Two to four minutes later the patient loses consciousness. 'They fall into a deep coma and they don't wake up. That's it,' Mr Minelli said.

The staff member returns later, checks the patient is dead by examining the pulse and pupils and dials 117, the Swiss police. The death is videotaped. When the police officer turns up, together with a coroner and a doctor, staff show them the tape to make clear that the suicide was voluntary. The tape is then erased.

The body is then taken to Zürich's Institute for Legal Medicine and from there is given to the family for cremation. The entire procedure – from Mr Minelli's living room to the crematorium – takes between three and five days.

Not everyone, though, is enamoured of Dignitas's methods, or Switzerland's growing reputation as a centre for 'suicide tourism'.

Andreas Brunner, a prosecutor for the canton of Zürich, has criticised Dignitas – saying that 'it is not good if Zurich becomes known as the city to die in', and has tried to introduce a new law which would make assisted suicide only available for people who have lived in Switzerland for six months.

Mr Brunner has also questioned whether some patients might re-consider their decision to take their lives, in different circumstances, and feel pressured to go through with the suicide once in Zürich.

Yesterday, however, Mr Minelli said he was equally happy for patients to turn around and go home – and said that some did.

Those who changed their mind included a 27-year-old Irishman with multiple sclerosis, whom Mr Minelli took to visit the grave of James Joyce and Zürich's botanical gardens; a clinically depressed young German; and an elderly woman from Munich,

## The law on euthanasia

*Netherlands*
In April 2002 became first country in world to sanction euthanasia.

*Belgium*
Law permitting voluntary euthanasia and assisted suicide passed May 2002.

*Switzerland*
Assisted suicide legal and does not require supervision of a doctor. Euthanasia illegal.

*Sweden*
No law specifically proscribing assisted suicide, but prosecutors can charge an assister with manslaughter.

*UK*
Up to 14 years' prison for assisting suicide. Law unclear on helping someone travel to country where they could receive help to end life.

*France*
Terminally ill patients will be given right to demand end to treatment under law before parliament.

*Germany*
Passive euthanasia permissible if patient clearly expresses wish to die.

*Oregon, US*
Passed Death with Dignity Act in 1994, becoming only US state to permit assisted suicide. Euthanasia illegal.

*Northern Territory, Australia*
Voluntary euthanasia law introduced in 1995, but federal parliament repealed it in 1997.

Linda MacDonald

whom he collected and drove back the same day.

What some supporters of the right to die find problematic, however, is that not all the people who come to the clinic are terminally ill, although all want to end their own lives. Mr Minelli yesterday admitted that a British couple who both died at his clinic might have lived longer, but had had enough.

Across Europe, meanwhile, attitudes towards PAS – or physician-assisted suicide – are changing. The Netherlands and Belgium have legalised euthanasia, while Sweden, Finland and Norway don't always prosecute physicians who help terminally ill patients to die.

Earlier this summer a House of Lords select committee invited Mr Minelli to give evidence, while considering a bill by Lord Joffe to permit assisted dying for the terminally ill.

Mr Minelli became interested in the right to die issue after visiting his maternal grandmother on her deathbed.

'When she asked the doctor if he could hasten her suffering, he refused,' he said. Mr Minelli refuses

to talk to all British journalists on principle because of the bad publicity from some tabloids, which have dubbed him Dr Death.

But he cites several British authorities for his cause, most notably Thomas More, who in 1517 wrote that people suffering unbearable physical torment had a right to end their life.

Last night Mr Minelli also pointed out that everybody dies – though they are often reluctant to recognise this fact. 'We know that we die, but nobody believes it's going to happen to them. We need to rescue this topic and talk about it at the family table. After all, we are all terminally ill,' he added, with a smile. 'Life is an illness spread by sexual contact. You die at the end 100%.'

■ The following correction was printed in the *Guardian*'s Corrections and clarifications column, Tuesday 7 December 2004.

In the article below, we refer to 'Mrs Z', saying that she has an incurable brain disease. In fact, events had overtaken our report. 'Mrs Z' died in Switzerland on 1 December.

© *Guardian Newspapers Limited 2004*

# 'I don't want to plan my death, I want to enjoy life'

**Britain is one of the few European countries where assisting suicide is still a crime.
By Jamie Doward**

Debbie Purdy loves life. The 41-year-old from Bradford describes herself as an adrenalin junkie. In her time Purdy has jumped out of planes, climbed mountains, trekked through jungles and scuba-dived. These days her biggest buzz comes from walking unaided.

Purdy has suffered from chronic and progressive multiple sclerosis for a decade. 'I don't have relapses or remissions, I just get steadily worse,' she says breezily.

Recently she started dropping things, something that has made her think about her life – and her death. 'At some point I know I will not be able to handle drugs and take an overdose. Before that happens, I've got to make a decision: should I end my life now? When the pain becomes unbearable and I've lost my dexterity completely, I won't be able to do it myself.'

Purdy has every intention – and gives every indication – of being around for many years to come. But it is a question she urgently needs to address now so that she can concentrate on enjoying the rest of her life. 'I couldn't ask my husband to help me because there is the possibility that he would be jailed for it. It's going to be hard enough for him losing his wife – I couldn't ask him to risk being prosecuted.'

Assisting suicides carries a maximum 14-year sentence in Britain, one of the few European countries where it is still a crime. Purdy, like her 55,000 fellow members of the Voluntary Euthanasia Society, believes this is wrong. 'The only thing that will improve the quality of my life now is a change in the law, so I don't have to be thinking about what I'm going to have to do by myself. If that no longer becomes the biggest question in my life, then I can start thinking about overcoming the symptoms I cope with.'

She considered going to Holland, where euthanasia for the terminally ill has been legalised. But patients need to have been registered with a Dutch doctor for two years before they qualify for medical assistance that would bring their lives to an end.

Purdy's hopes for a law change look slim, at least for now. 'People want to bury their heads in the sand on this issue. The other day I heard Linford Christie say "oh they could find a cure". That's just grabbing at straws. That's denial.'

She says she understands people's objections to euthanasia. 'In no way do I want to make it compulsory for someone to have to participate in assisted dying but, on the other hand, I don't have a moral or religious problem with it. It would improve my life and I don't want others to disrespect my opinion, either.

'My doctor doesn't feel comfortable with euthanasia. Fair enough. But I should be able to find a doctor who does feel comfortable with it. It's the same with abortion. My doctor feels uncomfortable with abortion, but when someone is seeking an abortion they're allowed to ask for a doctor who is comfortable with it. We're just asking for the same rights. I don't want to plan my death. I want to enjoy my life.'

It is a wish that is echoed by a growing number of people in the UK who want the right to make the decision about when and how their lives should end.

Improvements in healthcare have created an ageing society, but with the consequence that more and more people are spending the last years of their lives in pain from crippling diseases.

The government's solution has been to promise more money for palliative care. But pro-euthanasia groups believe this does not go far enough. They have criticised successive UK governments for failing to follow their European counterparts and investigate the argument for clarifying the law on assisted dying.

The government's failure to do so is unsurprising. Death is rarely a vote winner and politicians are wary about antagonising the pro-life lobby, which has produced some powerful arguments against euthanasia.

The Christian Medical Fellowship, for example, makes a persuasive case that people with a terminal illness are vulnerable because they worry about the burden they place on their family. Legalising assisted dying could increase this pressure, the CMF believes.

But the government's reluctance to discuss euthanasia has confused an already complex area of law. The word has come to be a 'catch-all' term encompassing everything from mercy killings to doctors administering lethal drug doses to patients in a coma.

'The problem has been to get the debate into the public forum, one that will allow people to be honest about their experiences,' acknowledges Deborah Annetts, chief executive of the Voluntary Euthanasia Society.

Amid the lacuna, people have started to take the law into their own hands. The Switzerland-based group, Dignitas, claims to have helped 22 Britons with terminal illnesses die abroad. Hardly a month goes by now without a pensioner confessing to killing a partner who was in agonising pain.

The CMF rejects the claim that euthanasia is a solution to patients' distress. 'Meticulous research in palliative medicine has in recent years shown that virtually all unpleasant symptoms experienced in the process of terminal illness can be either relieved or substantially alleviated by techniques already available,' it suggests.

But this argument is rejected by many in the medical professions. Just over half of nurses questioned in 2003 said the law should be amended to allow health professionals to help terminally ill people die.

In 1996, 54 per cent of 1,000 doctors questioned in a survey said they were in favour of legalising physician-assisted suicide in specific circumstances. The same survey found 3 per cent of GPs had helped terminally ill patients to die. That number is likely to have increased after several recent high-profile campaigns. The case of Diane Pretty, the woman with motor neurone disease who lost her high court fight to have her husband help end her life, attracted widespread media interest.

Now, in the latest assault on the pro-life lobby, crossbench peer Lord Joffe is attempting to steer a private member's bill legalising assisted dying through the House of Lords. Under Joffe's proposals voluntary euthanasia would be made available to patients who have less than six months to live and who are in 'unbearable pain'. Their decision to hasten an end to their life would be accepted only after they had undergone psychiatric and medical examinations and had been given a 'cooling-off' period to allow them to change their mind. Tory peers vehemently oppose the bill which had attracted 100,000 submissions when its consultation process was completed earlier this month.

Few think Joffe's bill will make it to law. But it may come to be seen as an important step towards legalised euthanasia in Britain.

Evan Harris, Liberal Democrat MP for Oxford West and Abingdon, gave evidence to the committee in which he recalled seeing terminally ill patients pumped full of morphine to speed their demise when he was working as a doctor. Harris believes a change in the law is necessary to regulate a practice that clearly exists but remains hidden behind closed doors.

'Doctors are always reluctant to see any change in the doctor-patient relationship, but I don't think they would oppose it if it became law. They accept it's a matter for society,' Harris says.

Annetts believes the combination of an ageing population and an increasingly secular society will become a catalyst for change.

'Ultimately the government will have to engage with this issue. The great thing about the euthanasia debate is we all have a view. We are all going to die.'

■ This article first appeared in *The Observer*, 19 September 2004.

© *Guardian Newspapers Limited 2004*

# ProLife Party responds to poll

It is reported in an NOP World survey that if euthanasia remains illegal in Britain, half of the 790 respondents would, if they were suffering unbearably, consider travelling abroad to die.

'The claims made by the Voluntary Euthanasia Society (VES) are grossly misleading,' said Julia Millington of the ProLife Party. 'The use of the phrase "suffering unbearably" suggests that the question is really about very extreme cases of severe illness and pain when the results are actually being used to support the general principle of voluntary euthanasia.

'It is also reported that in the last two years only 22 Britons have utilised the services of the Swiss-based euthanasia-provider, Dignitas. Therefore, if an average of only 11 people out of the half a million who die in the UK every year actually travel abroad to die, one must conclude that either the results of the survey are deceptive or that the vast majority of dying patients are not "suffering unbearably".

'The survey also asks people whether they want "medically-assisted dying". What do most people understand by this? Do they realise that it refers to either a lethal injection or cocktails of barbiturates?

'The issues at stake here are extremely serious. This comes at a time when the VES are again highlighting the suffering of Reginald Crew who sadly felt that his life was of so little value that he ended it prematurely.

'The portrayal of Mr Crew's suffering was and continues to be very emotive. The footage seen at the time of his death painted a very bleak picture. What we are not being shown are the many patients who are benefiting from first-rate palliative care and who completely reject the idea of euthanasia.

'The VES would have us believe that the law would only apply in certain cases where specified criteria are satisfied. However, evidence from countries where euthanasia has been legalised, such as Holland, shows that it is not possible to prevent the boundaries from being expanded. When the law says that killing is the answer to suffering in some cases, it inevitably becomes the answer to all suffering.

'The ProLife Party is opposed to all forms of euthanasia. Surely the response of a compassionate society is to alleviate the pain, to love and comfort the patient and to try and restore a sense of self-worth until death comes naturally.'

© *ProLife Party, September 2004*

# Support for change of the law

## Results prove law is 'unsustainable' says first witness to historic lords committee

47 per cent of people say they are prepared to break the law if a loved one asked them for help to die, an NOP World survey has revealed.

The survey has been published on the first day of oral evidence by an historic select committee of the House of Lords on the Assisted Dying for the Terminally Ill Bill.

It shows huge public support for changing the law to give terminally ill people the right to request and receive medical assistance to die. 82% of the public said the law should be changed and only 11% thought it should not.

Among those who are not religious, support for changing the law is a staggering 95%. Among Protestants and Catholics it is 81%.

Deborah Annetts, Chief Executive of VES (Voluntary Euthanasia Society) will be the first witness before the Committee when it meets. She said,

'NOP World's survey shows the public's support is unwavering and has actually increased since Diane Pretty died.

'By saying they would be prepared to break the law if a terminally ill loved one asked them to, the public are sending a clear message to our law makers that the law needs reform. The choice they have is between secret, unregulated assisted dying and a regulated system with the strictest safeguards in the world.

'It is plain that a one-size-fits-all law that criminalises the compassionate as much as it does serial killers is unsustainable.'

The UK law was last examined in 1994. Since then, Belgium, Holland and Oregon have changed their laws to permit assisted dying in different ways, and three senior Peers who voted against this in 1994 have changed their minds about the issue: Baroness Flather; Baroness Mary Warnock and Baroness Jay.

## choice, dignity.

It was revealed in September 2004, that 50% of Britons would be prepared to go abroad to seek medical help to die if they were terminally ill. Lesley Close, whose brother John went to Switzerland for an assisted death in 2002, said,

'It is incredibly sad that by offering no choice at all, the law forces the most vulnerable people in our society into such extreme and agonising choices. People want the law changed and Lord Joffe's Bill offers a much better way of dealing with these issues.'

The results were consistent across age, social class, voting intentions, gender and region.

■ The above information is from the Voluntary Euthanasia Society's website which can be found at www.ves.org.uk Alternatively, see page 41 for their address details.

© 2004, *Voluntary Euthanasia Society (UK)*

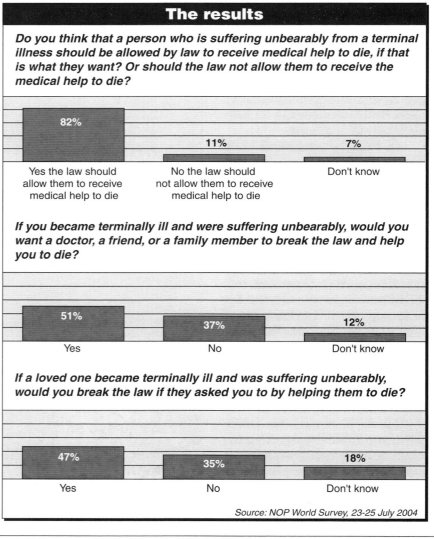

**The results**

Do you think that a person who is suffering unbearably from a terminal illness should be allowed by law to receive medical help to die, if that is what they want? Or should the law not allow them to receive the medical help to die?

| 82% | 11% | 7% |
|---|---|---|
| Yes the law should allow them to receive medical help to die | No the law should not allow them to receive medical help to die | Don't know |

If you became terminally ill and were suffering unbearably, would you want a doctor, a friend, or a family member to break the law and help you to die?

| 51% | 37% | 12% |
|---|---|---|
| Yes | No | Don't know |

If a loved one became terminally ill and was suffering unbearably, would you break the law if they asked you to by helping them to die?

| 47% | 35% | 18% |
|---|---|---|
| Yes | No | Don't know |

Source: NOP World Survey, 23-25 July 2004

# Disabled people want the right to die

## Four-fifths seek legalisation of euthanasia for the terminally ill, reveals a poll that suggests a big change in British attitudes

One of the final barriers to legalising euthanasia in Britain was shattered as it emerged that four-fifths of disabled people want the law changed so they can be helped to die if they become terminally ill.

The surprising finding is from a new opinion poll that suggests there has been a huge change in British attitudes to mercy killing.

For years disabled rights groups have fiercely resisted any move to legalise euthanasia, saying it would put their members at risk of abuse. Some even said such a change would encourage the disabled to commit suicide.

Now, however, the poll of 2,000 disabled people by research firm YouGov found that 80 per cent would back a bill allowing a rational disabled person with a terminal disease to be helped to die.

The poll's publication comes after a High Court judge refused to intervene in last week to stop the husband of a woman with a degenerative brain disease taking her to a clinic in Switzerland for an assisted suicide, even though the man could be committing a crime. It emerged that the 46-year-old woman committed suicide with an overdose of barbiturates at the Dignitas clinic in Zurich the following day.

According to the poll, 77 per cent of disabled people say the law on suicide discriminates against them, chiefly because they may be physically incapable of ending their lives on their own.

Anyone helping another person to commit suicide can now be prosecuted under UK law, though a ban on anyone attempting suicide was scrapped in 1961.

The poll, commissioned by the Voluntary Euthanasia Society

*By Jamie Doward and Jo Revill*

(VES), is a key plank in the case of campaigners backing Lord Joffe's private member's bill to allow doctors to help the terminally ill to die.

The campaigners say it shows huge popular support for relaxing the law. 'More than four in five disabled and older people support the Bill, and they believe the law discriminates against those who are least able to exercise choice,' said Deborah Annetts, the society's chief executive.

'That is why some are tragically driven to take their lives abroad. That is no sort of choice to face.

'This survey has removed the last objection to changing the law in this country – and it explodes the myth that the elderly and the disabled cannot speak for themselves. The people of Britain are demanding the law gives them more choice.'

But a spokeswoman for the Pro-Life Alliance, which campaigns against euthanasia, questioned the survey's validity and said society needed to focus on ways of making the last months of the terminally ill

bearable rather than examining ways to help them die.

'In a compassionate society there must be correct mechanisms of support in place. If you see someone standing on a bridge considering suicide you don't push them off. Euthanasia is giving them that push,' she said.

Last week's case made headlines when Mr Justice Hedley lifted an injunction banning the unidentified couple from going to Switerland, and left it to the police to decide what action to take.

Tara Flood, of the Disability Awareness in Action (DAA) group, told the parliamentary select committee studying the Joffe bill that the idea of Britain adopting similarly relaxed, Swiss-style laws on euthanasia was deeply troubling and could 'potentially create an open season for the killing of disabled people'.

She said a database kept by her group had recorded 16,300 violations against disabled people since 1990, nine per cent of which violated the right to life. Foreign companies offering assisted deaths to the terminally ill were running 'modern day death camps for disabled people'.

This week, a group of peers will visit the American state of Oregon to study a law which allows assisted dying. Terminally ill patients who are mentally competent can take a lethal dose of barbiturates in their home.

The Oregon Death with Dignity Act was passed six years ago and is seen as a model for the Joffe bill. Peers examining the Joffe proposals will meet doctors and politicians in Oregon, 10 December 2004.

■ This article first appeared in *The Observer*, 5 December 2004.

# Euthanasia

## Information from the Christian Medical Fellowship

### By Tim Maughan

The word 'euthanasia' comes from the Greek roots *eu* (well) and *thanatos* (death), but currently means much more than 'good-death'. Euthanasia has been usefully defined as 'the intentional killing, by act or omission, of a person whose life is felt not to be worth living'.[1] This is the definition that will be used here.

Euthanasia can be achieved either by acting deliberately, or by not taking an action deliberately. In either case a doctor's particular choice of action has ended a patient's life. This is justified on the basis that the person's life was 'not worth living', either in their own, or in someone else's assessment.

Before we look at the subject in more detail, it is important to establish three situations that should not be considered as euthanasia. First, stopping, or deciding not to initiate, a medically useless treatment is not euthanasia. A medically useless treatment is one where the suffering it causes would outweigh any benefits.

Secondly, giving treatments aimed at relieving pain and other symptoms when the treatment may also carry some risk of shortening life is not euthanasia; it is called 'double effect'.

Thirdly, competent people always have permission to refuse treatment and doctors cannot force them to have treatment against their will. If the person dies as a consequence the doctor is not performing euthanasia.

### The value of intent

The term passive euthanasia is used by some people to describe situations where a doctor deliberately allows a person to die. Some bioethicists say that in these situations 'killing' is the same as 'letting die'.[2] But the term 'passive euthanasia' is confusing.

The key issue is intention. Allowing terminally ill patients to die when there is nothing more that can be done to relieve their symptoms or treat their illness has long been part of good medical practice. Letting patients die when useful symptom-relief or treatment can be given is negligent.

Some argue that pain relief can shorten the lives of people with terminal cancer and therefore the doctor is actually aiding the patient's death. Under the doctrine of 'double effect' this is deemed ethically acceptable, since the doctor's intended outcome is pain relief and the unfavourable result of shortening life is not the intent.[3] In reality, successful pain relief can extend life as appetite and wellbeing improve.

The issue is that we normally place great value on intent. You can see it when we accept distinctions between manslaughter, negligence, crimes of passion and murder. In addition, intention is an important consideration when we make allowances for people with diminished responsibility. We don't just look at the outcome and simply apply a blanket punishment. We may even consider what alternatives were available.

If we ignore intent we are at risk of dehumanising ourselves. We effectively say that our motivations and intentions are not important and that all that matters are the outcomes, the products of our lives. If we do not consider intent when we discuss end-of-life decisions we dehumanise the doctor, turning him or her into little more than a technician who answers only to the wills of others.

> *The word 'euthanasia' comes from the Greek roots* eu *(well) and* thanatos *(death)*

### Pro-euthanasia voices

Arguments for euthanasia fall into three main categories: compassion, autonomy and economics.

#### Compassion

Many people fear that during a final illness they will have symptoms that cannot be treated, or that they will be 'kept alive' longer than they wish. The compassion argument is that letting people 'die with dignity' is kinder than forcing them to go on suffering.

This assumes that there are no treatments for the symptoms which prompt each request for euthanasia. In fact most physical symptoms such as pain and nausea can be reduced and in many cases effectively treated. This treatment may need to be managed by specialists in pain control or palliative care, and can be given in the community, in hospices or in dedicated hospital units.

Similarly, patients with motor neurone disease (a serious progressive neurological disorder) are often afraid of choking to death. But studies from the largest and most experienced hospice units have demonstrated that, with appropriate palliative care, this virtually never happens.[4] Some unpleasant effects of disease, like immobility and paralysis, may not be reversible, but people can still have meaningful lives.

Some symptoms are not physical and medicine alone cannot relieve the fears felt by people who have no hope beyond death. This is a very real issue, but it points to the need for spiritual as well as medical support for dying people. Real compassion will offer support in a way that can enable hope, bring meaning to life and give a new sense of empowerment in spite of suffering. Few patients request euthanasia when their physical, emotional and spiritual needs are properly catered for.

#### Autonomy

Autonomy is closely connected to the concept of human rights. The

1998 Human Rights Act established a list of fundamental 'rights' for every human being. These should not be impeded by anyone else.

Consequently some people argue for euthanasia on the basis that patients have a 'right to die'. For example in 2002 Diane Pretty, who had motor neurone disease, went to the European Court arguing that her right to die was an application of the right to life laid out in Article 2 of the Human Rights Act. The Court did not agree, ruling that Article 2's right to life did not include a right to choose when to end that life, and certainly not the right to demand help from someone else to end it. What is really being talked about by 'a right to die' is a right to have one's life ended – or more specifically the right to be killed by a doctor.

This has repercussions for doctors' rights and freedoms. A patient's right to die would impose on doctors a duty to kill.

Another intriguing consequence of giving doctors the power to kill could be the loss of a patient's autonomy. Vulnerable people could end up avoiding asking for medical help, for fear that their doctors would recommend euthanasia.

Autonomy is a powerful concept in western society, but the promise of being able to do 'whatever we want' is unrealistic. It is not possible to have complete autonomy, because our decisions impact other people. Inevitably others will be affected by an individual choosing to die.

### Economics
One argument is that we simply can't afford to keep people alive. It has been expressed by leading economists such as Jacques Attali, the former president of the European Bank for Reconstruction and Development, who said, 'As soon as he gets beyond 60-65 years of age, man lives beyond his capacity to produce, and he costs society a lot of money . . . euthanasia will be one of the essential instruments of our future societies.'[5]

In fact, the costs of terminal care are often exaggerated. Dying patients frequently just need good nursing care, and although this is labour intensive, the additional costs are not high even for those who

require medication. It is curative, rather than palliative, care that is expensive.

### Arguments against euthanasia
There are three key arguments against euthanasia: that it is unnecessary, dangerous and morally wrong.

### Unnecessary
Many believe that terminally ill people only have two options: either they die slowly in unrelieved suffering, or they receive euthanasia. In fact, there is a middle way, that of creative and compassionate caring.

Dying patients can be managed effectively at home or in the context of a caring in-patient facility.

A comparison between the UK and the Netherlands is informative. In the Netherlands euthanasia is accepted, and there is only a very rudimentary hospice movement. By contrast, a UK House of Lords committee in 1994 recommended that euthanasia should not be allowed and advised futher spending on the UK's already well-developed facilities to care specifically for people who are terminally ill.[6]

This is not to deny that there are patients presently dying in homes and hospitals who do not benefit from the latest advances in palliative care. But the solution to this is to make appropriate and effective care and training more widely available, rather than to provide for euthanasia. There is genuine concern that legalisation of euthanasia will reduce the quality and availability of palliative care.

### Dangerous
People with a terminal illness are vulnerable and lack the knowledge and skills to alleviate their own symptoms. They are often afraid about the future and anxious about the effect their illness is having on others. They can be depressed or have a false sense of worthlessness. They may be confused, or have dementia. It is very difficult for them to be entirely objective about their own situation.

Having the option of euthanasia is dangerous, because it would encourage vulnerable and potentially confused people to ask to die, rather than asking family, friends and society to take care of them.

Many elderly people feel a burden to family, carers and society. They may feel great pressure to request euthanasia 'freely and voluntarily'. Vulnerable people will be particularly sensitive to the suggestion that they are a burden on friends and relatives.

Additionally, an elderly person will be aware that they are using up financial and emotional resources and may be sad that their children's inheritance is dwindling; money that could help put their grandchild through university.

There is evidence that where euthanasia is legalised this pressure does occur. In the five years since the US state of Oregon legalised physician-assisted suicide, 35 per cent of patients receiving help to die said that feeling a burden on family, friends/caregivers was one of the reasons for their choice.[7] The question is, do we want a society where elderly and infirm people feel required to ask to die?

Vulnerable people need to hear that they are valued and loved. They need to know that we are committed first and foremost to their wellbeing, even if this does involve expenditure of time and money. The way we treat the weakest and most vulnerable people speaks volumes about the kind of society we are.

Chairman of the 1994 House of Lords Select Committee on Medical Ethics, Lord Walton of Detchant, explained their recommendation not to allow euthanasia as follows: 'We concluded that it would be virtually impossible to ensure that all acts of euthanasia were truly voluntary and that any liberalisation of the law in the United Kingdom could not be abused. We were also concerned that vulnerable people – the elderly, lonely, sick, or distressed – would feel pressure, whether real or imagined, to request early death.'[8]

Where voluntary euthanasia has been legalised and accepted, it has led to involuntary euthanasia. This has been demonstrated in the Netherlands[9] where, as early as 1990, over 1,000 patients were killed without their consent in a single year.

A report commissioned by the Dutch government showed that for 2001, in around 900 of the estimated 3,500 cases of euthanasia the doctor had ended a person's life without there being any evidence that the person had made an explicit request.[10]

In addition, when it came to reporting euthanasia there was a huge gulf between the expectation of Dutch law and actual practice. For example, only 54 per cent of doctors fulfilled their legal responsibility to report their actions concerning euthanasia. The researchers estimated that euthanasia accounted for 2.5 per cent of all deaths in the country. On average, five cases a year involve children.

Responding to the statistics, the Royal Dutch Medical Associa-tion was pleased that reporting had increased, but 'regretted' the number of doctors still not following the guidelines.

### Morally wrong
Traditional medical ethics codes have never sanctioned euthanasia. The Hippocratic Oath states 'I will give no deadly medicine to anyone if asked, nor suggest such counsel . . .'.

The 1949 International Code of Medical Ethics declares 'a doctor must always bear in mind the obligation of preserving human life from the time of conception until death'. In its 1992 Statement of Marbella, the World Medical Association confirmed that assisted suicide, like euthanasia, is unethical and must be condemned by the medical profession.

Medical practice is based on the ethic of preserving life and relieving suffering. The introduction of 'legalised death' into the doctor-patient relationship is likely to damage this relationship. Doctors may become hardened to death and to causing death and start to see their patients as disposable, particularly when they are old, terminally ill, or disabled. Reciprocally these vulner-able groups of people may start to doubt the intentions of their doctors. In the Netherlands disabled people already describe a growing mistrust of their doctors and fear of being admitted to hospitals[11] – which should be places of care and safety for the vulnerable members of society.

### The root problem
Diagnosing the root problem of a society that wants to kill its most frail and vulnerable members rather than care for them is a difficult and lengthy process, but euthanasia will not solve the problem. It will only add another symptom. Addressing over-interventionism, suffering and fear of death, by giving people ultimate control over the timing and mode of their death will not help the individuals, or society as a whole, to come to terms with the issues.

We should be addressing the all too often ineffective drives to maintain life at all costs. We need to analyse our attitudes to illness,

suffering and death. We should look at what it is to care for and respect our elderly members, and address the difficulties that they experience under current social structures. Ultimately we need to rediscover the virtues of responsibility and trust.

From the perspective of our health and beauty promoting society, the vision or anticipaton of serious illness is an awful prospect. People think that they would rather be dead than survive with severe disability. However, people in that condition have a different view of the situation. They have arrived there through a series of steps, gradually getting used to worsening health and coming to terms with their problems. At the same time they have a growing realisation that life, even in its restricted current form, is still a valuable thing. So, to the healthy onlooker, euthanasia seems to be a compassionate solution, whereas to the well-cared-for dying patient, life is still a wonder and something to be fought for.

### References
1. HOPE Leaflet. *Euthanasia is OK sometimes, isn't it?*
2. Steinbock B & Norcross A (eds). *Killing and Letting Die.* New York: Fordham University Press. 1994
3. Simon KM & Miller SA. Pain management at the end of life. *J Am Osteopath Assoc.* 2001; 19(10): 599-608
4. O'Brien et al. Motor neurone disease: a hospice perspective. *BMJ.* 1993; 304: 471-3
5. Quoted in: Salomon M. *L'avenir de la vie.* Paris: Seghers. 1981. p273-275
6. *Select Committee on Medical Ethics.* Report. London: HMSO 1994
7. Fifth Annual Report on Oregon's Death with Dignity Act. 6 March 2003
8. Walton. *Hansard.* 1994; May 9:1345
9. Remmelink Report. 1991. A translation is published in *Lancet.* 1991; 338:669-74
10. Sheldon T. Only half of Dutch doctors report euthanasia, study says. *BMJ.* 2003; 326: 1164
11. *The Telegraph.* 15 Oct 1998

■ The above information is from the Christian Medical Fellowship's website: www.cmf.org.uk

# The law is not working

## Voluntary Euthanasia Society (UK)

### choice, dignity.

### England and Wales

In England and Wales a person who assists in the suicide of another or an attempted suicide is liable to imprisonment for up to 14 years. Actively ending someone's life is treated as murder even if the person is suffering unbearably and has asked for assistance to die. The penalty for murder is a life sentence. The law makes no distinction as to whether the person who assists is a doctor or whether the person being helped is terminally ill and has made a considered decision he or she wants to end their life.

### The position in Europe

In Belgium, Switzerland, Germany, France, Sweden, Finland and, where assistance is provided by a medical practitioner, the Netherlands, assisted suicide is not an offence. In other countries such as Denmark and Norway, the penalties for such offences have been downgraded to as little as 60 days which is in sharp contrast to the penalty of 14 years in England and Wales.

Even countries which generally have more conservative social policies such as Spain, Portugal and Poland recognise that there may be situations in which someone wants help to die because of their medical condition. These predominantly Roman Catholic countries have addressed this issue by making special provision in their laws so that a person who ends someone's life at their request faces a lower penalty than is given for murder.

### What is the problem with UK law?

The problem with the law is two-fold. First, there is no legal framework in place which addresses the fact that some terminally ill people request assistance to die. If they do get help to die, those who assist are dealt with under the criminal law and face a charge of either murder or assisted suicide, neither of which is appropriate.

Secondly, there has been a failure on the part of the UK Government to address the fact that the law does not stop assisted dying taking place. Even though we have the most restrictive and inflexible law on assisted dying in Europe this does not stop doctors or relatives acting on the request of the terminally ill to help them to die. The criminal law does not work. It neither protects the vulnerable nor regulates assisted dying.

Irrespective of what the criminal law says, in every European country assisted dying takes place. In the UK too it is well known that patients ask for assistance to die and that members of the medical profession and relatives provide that assistance:

- 15% of UK doctors admitted to helping a patient to die at their own request (1998).[1]
- A 1997 survey[2] of 200 GPs found that 46.5% (93 GPs) had 'eased a patient's death in some way' irrespective that in some cases they were doing so against the law and without any form of regulation.
- A survey of over 750 GPs and hospital doctors in 1996[3] found that 3% had ended the lives of terminally ill patients at their request.
- 'There is an "unhelpful" gap between what the law says and what the law does.'

Michael Wilks, current Chairman of the British Medical Association Ethics Committee.[4]

The situation is the same in countries with strong Roman Catholic traditions: a survey of the Italian Society for Palliative Care in 1996[5] found that 39% of practitioners had received requests for help to die and 11.5% of those who had received such requests had complied at least once.

The criminal law does not effectively regulate assisted dying. Therefore another framework needs to be devised such as in Oregon (USA) or the Netherlands to regulate medical practice, protect the vulnerable, and provide the right for people with terminal illnesses to choose what in their personal opinion is a dignified death.

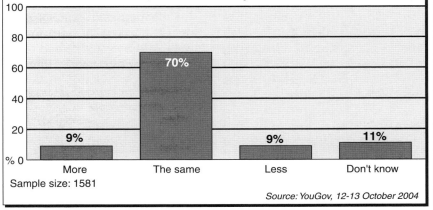

**Trust**

If the law were changed to allow, within strict guidelines, a terminally ill adult who was suffering unbearably to ask for and receive medication to end their life at a time of their choosing from their doctor, overall would you trust doctors . . . ?

| More | The same | Less | Don't know |
|------|----------|------|------------|
| 9% | 70% | 9% | 11% |

Sample size: 1581

Source: YouGov, 12-13 October 2004

## Changing the law to protect the vulnerable

At its root, it was the recognition by the Dutch Government that the criminal law was not protecting the patient or the doctor that resulted in the decriminalisation of assisted dying in the Netherlands.

The Dutch Government commissioned two national surveys, 'the Remmelink reports', which took place in 1990[6] and 1995.[7] These reports showed that in 1995, out of the 135,700 people who died, about 3,600 people died by virtue of 'voluntary euthanasia' or 'physician assisted suicide'. About 9,700 patients requested assistance to die. A third of these requests were rejected because they did not meet the requirements for help to die and another third did not persist in their requests and so died naturally.

Of those who received assistance to die, the most common disease from which the person was suffering was cancer. In 90% of assisted dying cases, life was shortened by one month or less, with 42% of cases involving the shortening of life by less than a week.

Following the work carried out by the Dutch Government, the Belgian Government commissioned similar research. The Belgian research[8] showed there was five times the level of 'non-voluntary euthanasia' (doctors ending the lives of patients without the latter requesting this) in Belgium than in the Netherlands. A similar conclusion was reached following research in Australia.[9]

The Belgian research showed that where there was no system of regulation less attention was given to careful end-of-life decision-making, putting the vulnerable at risk. Therefore for public policy reasons the Belgian Parliament voted in favour of legalising assisted dying to make sure medical practice is properly regulated so that everyone is protected.

In the UK we do not know how many deaths are as a result of assisted dying. We do not know how many non-voluntary assisted dying cases there are, although the evidence suggests that it may be as high as 18,000 per year. What we do know is that whatever the law says, both doctors and relatives will continue to break it out of compassion, to help ease the suffering people with terminal illnesses.

## Conclusion

### The law does not work:

- It fails to protect the vulnerable
- It does not recognise that assisted deaths go on irrespective of the fact that England and Wales have the harshest laws on the prevention of assisted dying in Europe
- It makes no distinction between murder or assisted suicide, and asking for help to die when you are terminally ill (unlike many other European countries)
- It denies those suffering unbearably from a terminal disease the right to choose medical assistance to die within proper legal safeguards

We need to have a full debate on what currently happens in the UK regarding end-of-life decision-making. We must put in place a system of regulation which protects the vulnerable, provides guidance and support to doctors, and facilitates choice for competent adults who are terminally ill and want to choose medical assistance to die.

### References

1  Doctor will you help me die? *The Sunday Times*, 15 November 1998.
2  GPs eased patients' deaths, *Pulse*, 1 November 1997.
3  Till death us do part, *BMA News Review*, 4 September 1996.
4  *BMA News Review*, 6 July 2002.
5  Di Mola G, Borsellino P, Brunelli C, Gallucci M, Gamba A, Lusignani M, Regazzo C, Santosuosso A, Tamburini M, and Toscani F, (1996), Attitudes toward euthanasia of physician members of the Italian Society for Palliative Care, *Annals of Oncology*, 7(9), 907-911.
6  Van der Maas PJ, van Delden JJM, Pijnenborg L, and Looman CWN, (1991), Euthanasia and other medical decisions concerning the end of life, *The Lancet*, 338, 669-674.
7  Van der Maas PJ, van der Wal G, Haverkate I, de Graaff CLM, Kester JGC, Onwuteaka-Philipsen BD, van der Heide A, Bosma J M, Willems D L, (1996), Euthanasia, physician-assisted suicide, and other medical practices involving the end of life in the Netherlands, 1990-1995, *New England Journal of Medicine*, 335, 1699-1705.
8  Deliens L, Mortier F, Bilsen J, Cosyns M, Stichele R V, Vanoverloop J, and Ingels K (2000) End-of-life decisions in medical practice in Flanders, Belgium: a nationwide survey, *The Lancet*, 356, 1806-1811.
9  Kuhse H, Singer P, Baume P, Clark M, and Rickard M, (1997), End-of-life decisions in Australian medical practice, *Medical Journal of Australia*, 166, 191-6.

- The above information is from the Voluntary Euthanasia Society's web site: www.ves.org.uk

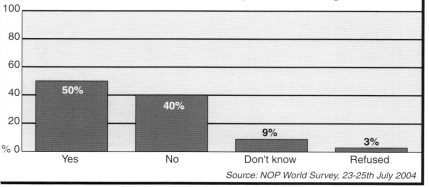

**Going abroad**

**If it remains illegal in the UK to ask for and receive medical help to die and you became terminally ill and were suffering unbearably, would you consider going abroad to receive assistance to die in a country where it is legal?**

| | Yes | No | Don't know | Refused |
|---|---|---|---|---|
| % | 50% | 40% | 9% | 3% |

*Source: NOP World Survey, 23-25th July 2004*

# Revealed: full scale of euthanasia in Britain

## Fury as number of 'assisted deaths' claimed to be 18,000

British doctors help nearly 20,000 people a year to die, according to one of the UK's leading authorities on euthanasia. The claim, the first public attempt by a credible expert to put a figure on 'assisted dying' rates, will reignite the emotive debate over the practice.

Dr Hazel Biggs, director of medical law at the University of Kent and author of *Euthanasia: Death with Dignity and the Law*, calculates that at least 18,000 people a year are helped to die by doctors who are treating them for terminal illnesses.

Biggs, who has submitted evidence to the House of Lords select committee which is examining Lord Joffe's private member's bill on Assisted Dying for the Terminally Ill, makes the claim in an article submitted to the *European Journal for Health Law*.

Her figures will place renewed focus on the doctor-patient relationship, which pro-euthanasia campaigners want changed so that medical staff can help conscious, terminally ill patients in pain to shorten their lives.

Biggs's figures are based on data from countries such as the Netherlands and Australia, which have published research into assisted dying rates, as well as evidence taken from British doctors.

'If you extrapolate from countries that have published data, you're looking at quite a large number of patients who may have had their end hastened, not necessarily with their consent,' she said.

'What this says to me is that we know these practices are going on, but they are completely unregulated. We don't know how many people are volunteers or non-volunteers, and

*By Jamie Doward,
Social Affairs Editor*

maybe because of that the law ought to be changed so that people can give voluntary consent, which will give them more protection.'

An ageing population has meant that an increasing number of doctors are taking private decisions to aid the early demise of terminally ill patients, usually by increasing drug doses.

Deborah Annetts, chief executive of the Voluntary Euthanasia Society, said there was an urgent need to clarify regulations governing assisted dying: 'We need to shine a spotlight on this. The medical profession doesn't want the public to realise they are making these decisions. It shows the need to make the patient the decision-maker. When it's left to the doctor, there is always the risk of abuse.'

Pro-euthanasia groups point out that in Britain the maximum sentence for helping someone to commit suicide is 14 years in prison. 'With the exception of Ireland, no other country in Europe behaves like that,' Annetts said.

Opinion polls show overwhelming public support for law changes that would make it easier for terminally ill patients in pain to request medical help to shorten their lives. In successive surveys, about 80 per cent of people back the move. A survey by the society this month found that 47 per cent of people said they were prepared to help a loved one to die, even if it meant breaking the law.

But a spokeswoman for the ProLife party said: 'Surely the response of a compassionate society is to alleviate the pain, to love and comfort the patient, and to try and restore a sense of self-worth until death comes naturally.'

Politicians have repeatedly deflected moves to change the law on euthanasia, believing it is unlikely to be a vote-winner. But Joffe's bill might find its way through the Lords committee stage and into the Commons, which would alarm religious groups.

In a joint submission to the select committee, Church of England and Roman Catholic bishops said: 'It is deeply misguided to propose a law by which it would be legal for terminally ill people to be killed or assisted in suicide by those caring for them, even if there are safeguards to ensure that only the terminally ill would qualify.'

■ This article first appeared in *The Observer*, 19 September 2004
© *Guardian Newspapers Limited 2004*

# The future of the right-to-die movement

## By Derek Humphry

When we look at what the right-to-die movement has achieved, against what it has wished to do, an honest person would agree that there is still a long, long way to go.

The first signs of organised activity on this issue came in the late 1930s in Britain, but nothing really happened until the 1970s when the public – the non-medical world – woke up with a shock to the fact that we often die differently nowadays compared to our ancestors.

This revelation – first made famous and characterized by the 'Karen Ann Quinlan pull-the-plug case in America' – brought a rush of legislation introducing the so-called 'Living Wills' – better known nowadays as Advance Directives, permitting the disconnection – or declining the use of – pointless life support equipment.

Today Advance Directives are available pretty well everywhere. That fight has largely been won, although the problem remains in getting people to appreciate their significance and sign them early enough before terminal ill health appears.

As this conference's information shows, Living Wills continually need to be improved to keep pace with medical advances and updated by the signators, even young people.

Where we have even further – much further – to go is related to active voluntary euthanasia and assisted suicide for the terminally ill adult, and the hopelessly ill person.

So far only the Netherlands and Belgium legally allow the first and second procedures, whilst Switzerland and Oregon (USA) allow assisted suicide. All the procedures mentioned here have strong rules and guidelines to prevent abuse.

Actually helping people who desire a hastened death so as to avoid further suffering has a long fight ahead of it. There is stiff opposition.

The underlying taboo in social life and the opposition of religious leaders in the rest of the Western world is holding back progress despite the knowledge that at a minimum – judging by electoral votes and opinion polls – fifty per cent of the general public wishes to see reform to give them an eventual certain death with dignity. Other opinion testings shows 70 to 80 per cent support for law reform.

The main problem is: how do we convert the converted into actual voters? The experience in America, probably the only place where actual citizens have on six occasions been asked to ballot for a right-to-die law, there are early indications that law reform will pass. Then, as the voters get to place their YEA or NAY on the ballot paper, many appear to have doubts. Except for the successful polls in Oregon in 1994 and 1996, the ballot initiatives have all failed.

Why is that? Many excuses have been offered, but my conclusion is that because we are not yet carrying a majority of the medical and nursing professions in support of us, the public – understandably – panics. Who amongst us is brave enough to defy our personal medical advisors?

Of course, not all doctors and nurses will ever support us. They are entitled to have religious and ethical differences. Yet only when we have a majority of them on our side – and saying so publicly – can we be assured that future law reform will succeed.

What must we do to bring more of the healing professions and their clients around to our way of thinking?

We have to change the climate of thinking in respect of individual choices in dying. We have to modify social changes ourselves. Others have done it in universal suffrage, birth control, marriage and divorces, abortion rights, and so on. Here is what I think we must do to start with:

First, be right there on the front line, at the bedside, for dying people who seek our help. Help comes in many different ways, from straightforward advice (which is my speciality), skilled counselling, and supervision of the justifiable suicide of a person who is dying, has fought all they could, and wants a careful release from this world.

The Dutch pioneered this 'at the home' approach from the 1970s onwards, and also the Swiss groups have admirable set-ups. Non-doctor assisted suicide is often the appropriate action in certain cases. On the West Coast of America, Compassion in Dying successful launched this type of personal compassion in the early 1900s, and Hemlock's 'Caring Friends' began similar work in 1999.

This kind of careful assistance, which comes in a multitude of ways depending on the patient's circumstances, is the most important way to build widespread voter confidence and trust. It takes time and effort but not only is it worth it to be responding to another human's cry for help, it earns admiration from a widening circle.

Secondly, if we are to eliminate the taboos and fears of abuse that some people have, we must make the subject of hastened death, assisted suicide, voluntary euthanasia – call it what you like – then we must get better integrated into our cultures.

For too long, the Judeo-Christian religions have dominated ethical thinking in the West. I am not learned enough to be sure, but it seems the same position obtains in the Buddhist, Muslim, Hindu, and other religions.

Our goals will only be achieved when there is more written about the subject in an investigative and compassionate way. We need to work for the day when the modern news media will report 'right-to-die' matters in a straightforward way and not wait for the 'scandal' and 'disgrace' incidents which they most love to report.

In sum, we must introduce our subject more healthily into literature, media and the arts so that is as commonplace to read, watch, or listen to, in our lives as watching sporting events or monitoring political news.

At least we cannot blame Hollywood, the movie industry, for ignoring us. In the last few years there have been four major movies dealing with rational suicide, and all were appropriate and tasteful.

Trouble is, they may run out of material unless concerned new writers emerge.

Thirdly, we need a few ordinary physicians in different countries to become involved in criminal proceedings: to be the 'guinea pigs' and the causes célebres. If politicians are nervous about our goals, then we should use the courts. But you cannot go to the courts without a defendant willing to take the heat and strain of a high-profile trial. Such martyrs are a rarity.

We need a few doctors who will stand up and say: 'My patient was suffering unbearably as he was dying. My patient was rational. I assisted a death on request. I will fight in the courts for my duty to help a patient.'

Dr Jack Kevorkian thought he was the man to shake the American medical profession into changing its attitude on euthanasia. But he failed, and some say did harm to the cause but other disagree. His public relations problems in respect to enhancing the attitudes to euthanasia were that he was a pathologist and not a general practitioner, and more of a showman than a mission-ary. More of a media circus performer than a dedicated campaigner. A loner not a team player. He alone thought he could alter the attitudes of the huge American medical profession. He underestimated the respect doctors have for the law of the land. Without law reform accompanying it, they would not take the same chances which he would.

---

*We need to work for the day when the modern news media will report 'right-to-die' matters in a straightforward way and not wait for the 'scandal' and 'disgrace' incidents*

---

Dr Kevorkian's final objective was right but his tactics proved to be wrong. But I give Kevorkian the credit for awakening millions of slumbering people to the very existence of assisted deaths.

Today he languishes in an American prison, convicted on his own evidence of murder, serving ten

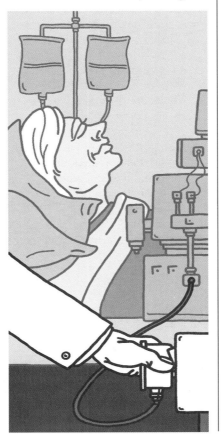

years to life. At 76 he may never see liberty again. For all his courage and unswerving dedication he has paid dearly. His legal advisors are now seeking a clemency deal, and I really hope they succeed. The predicament in thinking about Dr Kevorkian is that, while legally he was 100 per cent guilty of euthanising Thomas Youk, who was dying, because he video-taped it, is that 'murder' in the usual sense of the term?

Unfortunately, Anglo-American law makes no distinction on these grounds: 'A person cannot ask to be killed.' We must get this modified.

My plea is for the laws on homicide to be changed to allow somebody accused of a 'mercy killing' to at least plead justification and necessity. Not an automatic, knee-jerk excuse but a factual plea for understanding of the circumstances. Currently no such evidence or witness can be entertained. In my view we should work for a wider interpretation of the laws on death and dying and not just 'assisted suicide'.

In closing my remarks, please allow me to make a plea for more honest use of words and phrases throughout our movement. In recent years there has been a obvious backing away from words like 'euthanasia' and 'assisted suicide' and 'mercy killing'. I am quite aware that this was done for political correctness, trying not to scare off the politicians and the voters.

But not calling 'a spade a spade' – as the English say – is playing into the hands of our opponents, who increasingly are teasing us that we are more sinister than we say we are. Speaking in euphemisms – softened speech – develops into muddled thinking and mistaken actions.

I hope we all here are – as I am – fighting for the ultimate civil liberty, the right to choose to die when we wish and how we wish, no matter what it is called.

■ The text of this article was taken from a speech by Derek Humphry at the 15th World Conference, Tokyo 2004 (September 2004). For more information visit www.finalexit.org

© Derek Humphry 2004

# Medically assisted dying in the UK

## Information from the Voluntary Euthanasia Society

**choice, dignity.**

Surveys of healthcare professionals show a significant number admit to helping patients to die at their own request regardless of what the current law says.

Some of this data is difficult to interpret since it cannot be assumed that the respondents share the same understanding and definitions of terms such as 'euthanasia'. Nevertheless the published surveys do provide evidence that some healthcare professionals are willing to disregard the law. This is a view supported by Professor Griffiths[1] who highlights and criticises the UK legal system for effectively denying what regularly takes place in clinical practice.

Unlike Italy, Switzerland, Denmark, Belgium, Sweden, Norway, the Netherlands and Australia, the British Government has never, and refuses to, commission research into the frequency of assisted dying in the United Kingdom.

This research is vital to ensure healthcare and social care professionals and most importantly patients, are protected during end-of-life decision making.

### UK doctors are helping patients die

15% of UK doctors admit to helping a patient to die at their own request (1998)[2]

Medix-uk.com on-line survey of 1,002 UK doctors from all specialities (January 2003)

- 55% of doctors thought a person who has a terminal illness and uncontrollable physical suffering should be allowed to request physician assisted suicide
- 40% of doctors had been asked by a patient to assist in their suicide or euthanasia
- The doctors questioned covered at least 2,168 patients with untreatable and debilitating long-term or terminal illness and 55 (2.5%) of those patients had committed or attempted suicide in the last 6 months
- 46% of doctors with patients with untreatable and debilitating long-term or terminal illness had at least one patient who indicated that they would prefer to die than remain alive

A 1997 survey[3] of 200 GPs found that

- 46.5% had 'eased a patient's death in some way'
- 49% had been in a position where they felt that easing a patient's death – other than with the specific intention of relieving symptoms only – was the right course of action

A survey of 1,000 medical practitioners in 1996[4] found that

- 54% were in favour of legalising Physician Assisted Suicide in specific circumstances
- 28% had been asked to assist a patient to die
- 4% had assisted a patient to die

A survey of over 750 GPs and hospital doctors in 1996[5] found that

- 46% agreed that 'doctors should be legally permitted to actively intervene to end the life of a terminally ill patient where the patient, when mentally competent, has made a witnessed request for euthanasia'
- 37% would help terminally ill patients to die if it were legal
- 3% of GPs had helped terminally ill patients to die

In a survey of NHS doctors in 1994[6]

- 32% confirmed they had complied with a request from a patient to hasten their death

### Quotes from Chairmen of the British Medical Association Ethics Committee

'If we genuinely believe that all the efforts of medicine have been exhausted it may well be that in a particular case euthanasia has to be considered. That is a matter for the doctor concerned and I would be the last person to say they had done the wrong thing'

Dr Stuart Horner, Chairman in 1996.[7]

'There is an "unhelpful" gap between what the law says and what the law does.'

Michael Wilks, current Chairman of the British Medical Association Ethics Committee.[8]

## 2002 BMA Conference motion on Assisted Dying

The 2002 annual British Medical Association (BMA) conference in Harrogate voted on a motion calling for the 1961 Suicide Act to be amended so that mentally competent individuals who are physically incapable of ending their own life could have assistance to die.

'This meeting believes in the light of the case of Diane Pretty and others that amendment of the Suicide Act is necessary and desirable to take account of mentally competent individuals who wish to take their own lives but are physically incapable of so doing.'

■ 46% of doctors voted for this motion.

### References

1 Griffiths P, (1999), Physician-assisted suicide and voluntary euthanasia: is it time the law caught up? *Nursing Ethics*; 6 (2), 107–117.
2 Doctor will you help me die? *The Sunday Times*, 15 November 1998.
3 GPs eased patient's deaths', Pulse, 1 November 1997.
4 McLean S A M and Britton A, (1996) *Sometimes a small victory*, Institute of Law and Ethics in Medicine, University of Glasgow.
5 Till death us do part, *BMA News Review*, 4 September 1996.
6 Ward B J and Tate P A, (1994), Attitudes among NHS doctors to requests for euthanasia, *British Medical Journal*, 308, 1332-1334.
7 *BMA News Review*, 5 September 1996.
8 *BMA News Review*, 6 July 2002.
9 Survey support for euthanasia law, *Nursing Times*, 99 (5).
10 The euthanasia debate: how NT readers view the issues, *Nursing Times*, 91 (35), 36-38.

■ The above information is from the Voluntary Euthanasia Society's website which can be found at www.ves.org.uk

## Nurses support a change in the law

Surveys of UK nurses are scarce. However those carried out tend to confirm the experiences of other members of medical teams. Nurses appear to have greater exposure to patients expressing their wishes at the end of their lives. Perhaps this explains why they appear to be even more sympathetic to a change in the law than doctors. *Nursing Times* magazine has conducted a number of surveys:

*1. An online survey in 2003[9] showed that one in twenty nurses think colleagues are helping terminally ill patients to die and that well over half (at least 59%) support a change in the law to allow terminally ill patients the option of choosing an assisted death. 1,173 nurses were asked:*

'Should UK laws be changed to allow health professionals and relatives to help terminally ill patients end their lives with dignity?' They replied:

| | |
|---|---|
| Possibly, but clear guidelines | 51% |
| No, all human life sacred | 36% |
| Yes, it is inhumane to force needless suffering on patients | 8% |
| Health professionals already quietly help patients to die | 5% |

*2. In 1995, Nursing Times[10] asked 150 nurses the following questions:*

'Has anyone in your area ever requested euthanasia?'

| | |
|---|---|
| Yes | 69% |

'To whom was it made?'

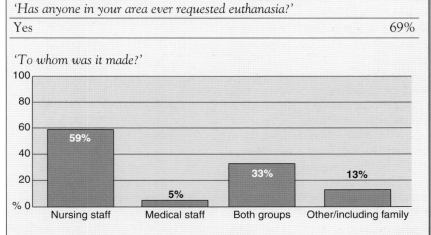

'Has a member of medical staff ever requested your participation in performing euthanasia?'

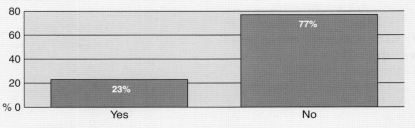

'Do you believe that requests for euthanasia should be granted?'

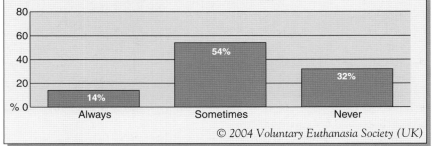

# Assisted suicide

## Information from the World Federation of Right to Die Societies

### What is physician-assisted suicide (PAS)?

Physician-assisted suicide (PAS) generally refers to a practice in which the physician provides a patient with a lethal dose of medication, upon the patient's request, which the patient intends to use to end his or her own life.

### Is physician-assisted suicide the same as euthanasia?

No. Physician-assisted suicide refers to the physician providing the means for death, most often with a prescription. The patient, not the physician, will ultimately administer the lethal medication. Euthanasia generally means that the physician would act directly, for instance by giving a lethal injection, to end the patient's life. Some other practices that should be distinguished from PAS are:

- Terminal sedation: This refers to the practice of sedating a terminally ill competent patient to the point of unconsciousness, then allowing the patient to die of her disease, starvation, or dehydration.
- Withholding/withdrawing life-sustaining treatments: When a competent patient makes an informed decision to refuse life-sustaining treatment, there is virtual unanimity in state law and in the medical profession that this wish should be respected.
- Pain medication that may hasten death: Often a terminally ill, suffering patient may require dosages of pain medication that impair respiration or have other effects that may hasten death. It is generally held by most professional societies, and supported in court decisions, that this is justifiable so long as the primary intent is to relieve suffering.

### Is physician-assisted suicide ethical?

The ethics of PAS continue to be debated. Some argue that PAS is ethical (see arguments in favour). Often this is argued on the grounds that PAS may be a rational choice for a person who is choosing to die to escape unbearable suffering. Furthermore, the physician's duty to alleviate suffering may, at times, justify the act of providing assistance with suicide. These arguments rely a great deal on the notion of individual autonomy, recognising the right of competent people to choose for themselves the course of their life, including how it will end.

> *Often a terminally ill, suffering patient may require dosages of pain medication that impair respiration or have other effects that may hasten death*

Others have argued that PAS is unethical (see arguments against). Often these opponents argue that PAS runs directly counter to the traditional duty of the physician to preserve life. Furthermore, many argue if PAS were legal, abuses would take place. For instance, the poor or elderly might be covertly pressured to chose PAS over more complex and expensive palliative care options.

### What are the arguments in favour of PAS?

Those who argue that PAS is ethically justifiable offer the following sorts of arguments:

- Respect for autonomy: Decisions about time and circumstances of death are very personal. Competent person should have right to choose death.
- Justice: Justice requires that we 'treat like cases alike'. Competent, terminally ill patients are allowed to hasten death by treatment refusal. For some patients, treatment refusal will not suffice to hasten death; only option is suicide. Justice requires that we should allow assisted death for these patients.
- Compassion: Suffering means more than pain; there are other physical and psychological burdens. It is not always possible

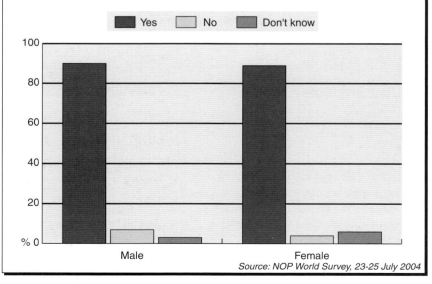

**Pain relief**

**Do you think that a terminally ill patient should have a right to ask for and receive sufficient pain relief as judged by them, if they want it?**

Legend: Yes | No | Don't know

*Source: NOP World Survey, 23-25 July 2004*

to relieve suffering. Thus PAS may be a compassionate response to unbearable suffering.

- Individual liberty vs. state interest: Though society has strong interest in preserving life, that interest lessens when person is terminally ill and has strong desire to end life. A complete prohibition on assisted death excessively limits personal liberty. Therefore PAS should be allowed in certain cases.

- Openness of discussion: Some would argue that assisted death already occurs, albeit in secret. For example, morphine drips ostensibly used for pain relief may be a covert form of assisted death or euthanasia. That PAS is illegal prevents open discussion, in which patients and physicians could engage. Legalisation of PAS would promote open discussion.

### What are the arguments against PAS?

Those that argue that PAS should remain illegal often offer arguments such as these:

- Sanctity of life: This argument points out strong religious and secular traditions against taking human life. It is argued that assisted suicide is morally wrong because it contradicts these beliefs.

- Passive vs. active distinction: The argument here holds that there is an important difference between passively 'letting die' and actively 'killing'. It is argued that treatment refusal or withholding treatment equates to letting die (passive) and is justifiable, whereas PAS equates to killing (active) and is not justifiable.

- Potential for abuse: Here the argument is that certain groups of people, lacking access to care and support, may be pushed into assisted death. Furthermore, assisted death may become a cost-containment strategy. Burdened family members and health care providers may encourage option of assisted death. To protect against these abuses, it is argued, PAS should remain illegal.

- Professional integrity: Here opponents point to the historical

ethical traditions of medicine, strongly opposed to taking life. For instance, the Hippocratic oath states, 'I will not administer poison to anyone where asked,' and 'Be of benefit, or at least do no harm.' Furthermore, major professional groups (AMA, AGS) oppose assisted death. The overall concern is that linking PAS to the practice of medicine could harm the public's image of the profession.

- Fallibility of the profession: The concern raised here is that physicians will make mistakes. For instance there may be uncertainty in diagnosis and prognosis. There may be errors in diagnosis and treatment of depression, or inadequate treatment of pain. Thus the State has an obligation to protect lives from these inevitable mistakes.

### Is PAS illegal?

In most nations and in most states in the US, aiding in a suicide is a crime. However, suicide or attempted suicide itself is not illegal, although an attempted suicide will often result in a short-term involuntary psychiatric commitment for a psychiatric assessment and evaluation. The state of Oregon is the only state within the United States that currently has legalised PAS. A constitutional

---

*Surveys of patients and members of the general public find that the vast majority think that PAS is ethically justifiable in certain cases*

---

challenge to the Washington State law was dismissed by the US Supreme Court in 1997, with the court refusing to recognise PAS as a constitutional right. The Supreme Court left it to individual states to address the legality of PAS through legislation, but encouraged efforts to improve care of the dying.

Despite the apparent illegality of PAS in most states, no physician has ever been convicted for PAS. Dr Timothy Quill was investigated but not indicted for his participation in the suicide of a patient after he published his account of the incident. Jack Kevorkian was convicted for second degree murder for an act that more closely approximated active euthanasia.

### What does the medical profession think of PAS?

Surveys of individual physicians show that half believe that PAS is ethically justifiable in certain cases. However, professional organisations such as the American Medical Association have generally argued against PAS on the grounds that it undermines the integrity of the profession.

Surveys of physicians in practice show that about 1 in 5 will receive a request for PAS sometime in their career. Somewhere between 5 and 20% of those requests are eventually honoured.

### What do patients and the general public think of PAS?

Surveys of patients and members of the general public find that the vast majority think that PAS is ethically justifiable in certain cases, most often those cases involving unrelenting suffering.

### What should a physician do if a patient asks him or her for assistance in suicide?

One of the most important aspects of responding to a request for PAS is to be respectful and caring. Virtually every request represents a profound event for the patient, who may have agonised over his situation and the possible ways out. The patient's request should be explored, to better understand its origin, and to determine if there are other interventions that may help ameliorate the motive for the request. In particular, one should address:

- motive and degree of suffering: are there physical or emotional symptoms that can be treated?
- psychosocial support: does the patient have a system of psycho-social support, and has she discussed the plan with them?
- accuracy of prognosis: every consideration should be given to acquiring a second opinion to verify the diagnosis and prognosis.
- degree of patient understanding: the patient must understand the disease state and expected course of the disease. This is critical since patient may misunderstand clinical information. For instance, it

is common for patients to confuse 'incurable' cancer with 'terminal' cancer.

**What if the request persists?**
If a patient's request for aid-in-dying persists, each individual clinician

must decide his or her own position and choose a course of action that is ethically justifiable. Careful reflection ahead of time can prepare one to openly discuss your position with the patient, acknowledging and respecting difference of opinion when it occurs. Organisations exist which can provide counselling and guidance for terminally ill patients. No physician, however, should feel forced to supply assistance if he or she is morally opposed to PAS.

- The above information is from the World Federation of Right to Die Societies' website which can be found at www.worldrtd.net

© *The World Federation of Right to Die Societies*

# Swiss charity says its clients 'die with dignity'

*By David Derbyshire*

About two dozen terminally-ill Britons are thought to have travelled to Switzerland as 'suicide tourists' in the last few years.

All have been clients of Dignitas – a charity set up in 1998 with the slogan 'live with dignity, die with dignity'.

The Swiss law on suicide states that helping someone to die 'out of a self-interested motivation' is punishable by up to five years in prison.

Although it does not explicitly state that other forms of voluntary euthanasia are legal, authorities have allowed Dignitas and three other organisations to offer the service.

Switzerland has the greatest number of cases of assisted suicides in Europe, according to a report by Zurich University.

Assisted suicide is also permitted in Holland, Belgium and the state of Oregon in America.

In 1996, Australia's Northern Territory legalised voluntary euthanasia. Bob Dent, a terminally-ill cancer patient, was the first to use the law with a lethal dose administered by a voice-controlled computer. Three more people died

until the law was overturned by the federal government two years later.

Dignitas is the most controversial of the Swiss voluntary suicide organisations. It is the only one to offer help to foreigners and, until December 2004, was the only one that offered voluntary euthanasia to the mentally ill.

*Switzerland has the greatest number of cases of assisted suicides in Europe, according to a report by Zurich University*

Reginald Crew, of Hunt's Cross, Liverpool, was one of the first Britons to get help from Dignitas to end his life.

Mr Hunt, 74, died in January 2003 after taking barbiturates. He

had been suffering from motor neurone disease for five years.

The charity, which is run by Ludwig Minelli, a lawyer, also helped a British couple, Robert and Jennifer Stokes, to end their lives in 2003. Neither was thought to be terminally ill but were suffering from mental illness and chronic diseases and were in constant pain.

In September, Lesley Close, whose brother John had used the Zurich group to end his life, said 22 Britons had been given help from Dignitas. She said the organisation had more than 550 members in Britain.

Last year, the public prosecutor's office in Zurich said it was investigating some of the cases in which the charity had helped people to die.

Dignitas claims its staff are volunteers – which gets around the ban on self-interested motivation. Clients sign a document stating that the decision is theirs alone and always make the last act – either swallowing a drug or opening the valve of a drip.

© *Telegraph Group Limited, London 2004*

# Secret killings of newborn babies

**Secret killings of newborn babies trap Dutch doctors in moral maze. Call for new rules to end dilemma for medical and legal professions**

Once a month on average somewhere in the Netherlands a doctor injects a newborn baby with a lethal cocktail of morphine and sedatives. Within a few hours, the baby is dead. The agonising decision is taken, invariably at the pleading of distraught parents, because the infant is born into excruciating pain with life-threatening illness or disability and with little or no prospect of recovery or successful treatment.

Routinely, the killings are carried out in secret. The reasons for the deaths are covered up. The death certificates the doctors are obliged to fill out are falsified in order to render the doctors immune to prosecution for murder.

'We know these cases are happening every year. There's a kind of consensus that it is justifiable,' says Johan Legemaape, legal adviser to the Royal Dutch Medical Association. 'But it's still a very sensitive subject and it raises a strong reaction.'

The moral, psychological and emotional pressures raised by the topic of killing infants are daunting in the extreme, and in Holland, which has allowed strictly controlled euthanasia for 10 years, doctors are now demanding new rules governing the practice.

'It's time to be honest about the unbearable suffering endured by newborns with no hope of a future,' said Dr Eduard Verhagen, head of paediatrics at Groningen hospital, in a statement in December 2004. 'All over the world doctors end lives discreetly out of compassion without any kind of regulation. This is a subject that nobody likes to acknowledge, let alone discuss.'

Behind the scenes paediatricians in the Netherlands have been making tacit deals with local

*By Ian Traynor in Nijmegen, the Netherlands*

prosecutors' offices for years, promising to report cases of 'life-ending treatment for newborns' in return for guarantees that the doctors will not find themselves hauled into the dock facing charges of murder.

## 'It's time to be honest about the unbearable suffering endured by newborns with no hope of a future'

Last year Dr Verhagen's clinic in Groningen carried out three terminations of newborns and reported the cases to the prosecutor's office, which decided not to bring charges.

Leendert De Lange, an official at the national prosecutor's office in The Hague, says there have been 18 such cases of 'neo-natal' deaths reported to the judicial authorities in the past four years, none of them resulting in prosecution.

The doctors say this is about one-third of the total number of such cases, with most cases going unreported because of the doctors' fears.

Two test cases in the mid-90s set the precedent. Two doctors, one a neurologist, the other a GP, reported the killing of two newborns and were tried for murder. They were acquitted and appeal courts in both cases confirmed the acquittals. Since then there have been no more trials.

'In fact the prosecutors are not prosecuting these cases,' says Professor John Griffiths, author of the 1997 book, *Euthanasia and Law in the Netherlands*, and an expert in euthanasia law at the University of Groningen, in the north-east of the country.

Such a situation is not good enough for Dr Louis Kollée, the head of paediatrics at the Radboud University Medical Centre in the eastern Dutch town of Nijmegen.

Along with a bunch of like-minded colleagues from children's and maternity wards across the Netherlands, Dr Kollée is campaigning for new rules surrounding the killing at birth of babies whose condition is so serious that they

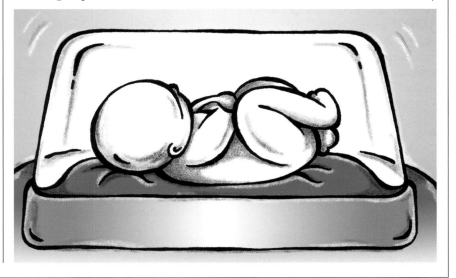

cannot be expected to survive for long.

'If the doctor and the parents decide to terminate the life of the baby, it is illegal, in any country. So it is murder,' says Dr Kollée. 'This is all very problematic for a doctor. He feels like a criminal. It's very difficult.'

Dr Kollée and his colleagues argue that they want neither to legalise nor to decriminalise the lethal injections administered by doctors into newborns. But they want a new system of government-endorsed regulation that will minimise the chances of prosecution.

Professor Griffiths says this is a contradictory position, that the practice can only either be legal or illegal. 'And if it's illegal, it can only be murder.'

But the paediatrics lobby has taken legal advice and is confident that its campaign can succeed.

A 15-page protocol drafted by the doctors and their lawyers last September calls for government action on their concerns and for the formation of a new national commission to seek a way out of the moral maze.

The increasingly public debate over how to handle such distressing cases – Dr Verhagen gives the example of a newborn with hydrocephalus and no brain or of a child born with spina bifida 'with a sack of brain fluid attached where all the nerves are floating around' – opens up *terra incognita* in a country at the forefront of the global debate on euthanasia.

Euthanasia has been practised for 10 years in the Netherlands, the first country in the world to legalise the practice, and now accounts for 4-5,000 deaths a year, 3.5% of the national death rate.

The practice is severely circumscribed and tightly regulated. It is estimated that doctors in the Netherlands, the only people allowed to perform euthanasia, turn down two-thirds of euthanasia requests.

Euthanasia is legal from the age of 12. It cannot apply to children because they cannot take a free decision. But several moves are afoot to extend euthanasia beyond the current limits.

For example, a national commission of experts concluded in

December 2004 after three years of deliberation that euthanasia rights should be extended to those wanting to die because they are 'tired of life'. There is also a discussion about euthanasia for patients suffering from dementia, as well as about psychiatric and other cases involving patients unable to take a rational decision for themselves.

On top of these debates comes the discussion over newborns. The dilemma has triggered surprisingly little debate in the Netherlands, but has caused a storm of controversy outside, particularly among the religious right in the US and in the churches.

'From the point of view of the Netherlands, this debate about newborns is a logical development,' says Professor Henk Jochemsen, a medical ethicist and Christian critic of euthanasia. 'It's another step in the wrong direction.'

Bishop Elio Sgreccia, of the Vatican's Pontifical Academy for Life, has written to the paediatricians to voice outrage at the proposals, likening them to the Nazis' mass murder of 70,000 physically and mentally disabled under the euphemism of euthanasia.

---

*Euthanasia is legal from the age of 12. It cannot apply to children because they cannot take a free decision*

---

The Vatican accusations, in turn, caused great distress to the paediatricians who argue that they are only seeking to bring into the open what is already established practice, and not only in the Netherlands.

'It's not good that these very delicate and difficult decisions are done secretly,' says Jost Wessel, a spokesman for the hospital in Groningen.

Dr Kollée says: 'We want doctors who end the life of a baby to report the cases and that the cases are properly reviewed. The great majority of paediatricians have told us that these end-of-life decisions should be properly examined and not practised in the dark.'

The paediatricians say that up to 15 children are killed at birth every year in the Netherlands and that worldwide the figure is around 600 a year. Professor Jochemsen worries about the implications of a favourable government response to the pressure from the paediatricians.

'These doctors say it is restricted to very clear diagnoses. But practice tells us it will be gradually extended to others. What is being considered now couldn't have been considered 10 years ago. It's the slippery slope.'

Dr Kollée contends the very opposite: 'If the practice is not controlled and regulated, then we will end up on the slippery slope. We don't want this type of decision to become easy. We don't want to increase the number of patients whose lives are terminated. It must be exceptional. It shouldn't be done. But sometimes a doctor can't do anything else.'

© *Guardian Newspapers Limited 2004*

# Professionals speak

It is often said and endlessly repeated that because the British Medical Association and the Royal College of Nursing have not pressed for the law to be changed, the vast majority of nurses and doctors oppose a change in the law.

In fact, many healthcare professionals in the UK support/are neutral towards assisted dying; and if legal would be willing to be involved

The Medix-UK survey in 2003 found 55% of physicians thought assisted dying should be permitted when a patient has a terminal illness with uncontrollable suffering.

The ORB survey asked physicians what they thought about 'euthanasia' and 'assisted suicide'. 61% opposed 'euthanasia' and 60% opposed 'assisted suicide'. However, the question was not put in the context of helping a patient to die who was terminally ill, suffering unbearably and had asked for help to die. Despite this, 23% (administering medication) to 26% (prescribing medication only) of physicians would be prepared to assist a patient to die were it legal to do so.

A recent *Nursing Times* survey (Hemmings 2003) found that two out of three nurses thought there should be legislation for assisted dying; one in four had been asked by a patient to help them end their life. This finding is particularly important given that nurses spend the most time with patients, and patients often speak to nurses first (i.e. before physicians) about their request for assistance to die (De Beer et al in press; van de Scheur and van der Arend 1998)

Notably, the editorial of the journal *Lancet Neurology* (Oct 2003) stated:

'There is a clear mismatch between what the general public and doctors' organisations perceive to be acceptable. Physicians have the right to refuse to assist a patient to die if their conscience prevents them from doing so. But mentally competent terminally ill patients should also have the right to choose when, where, and how they die. Importantly, physician-assisted suicide should never become commonplace and must always be the exception, not the rule. Legislation is urgently needed to ensure that by upholding a patient's right to die, other members of society are not compromised. Lord Joffe's Bill should be supported.'

---

### 'There is a clear mismatch between what the general public and doctors' organisations perceive to be acceptable'

---

Perhaps the most compelling evidence comes from health professionals themselves. Here are some of the quotes we have received.

'I have seen patients with intractable pain and progressive disease who do not want to suffer any more – it is a fallacy that palliative care can adequately control all symptoms in all patients.' – Doctor

'The moment of death may be distressing, but the process of dying can be unbearably painful for victim and family. I find it difficult to argue against bringing forward the inevitable in such circumstances.' – Doctor

'When a British citizen has to go to Switzerland to end his life (motor neurone disease) it makes one realise how backward we are in the UK.' – Doctor

'It is barbaric that I can treat my dog/cats better than my relatives/ patients in these circumstances. I despise those who wish to inflict their (often religious) views on others to prevent access to a dignified end-of-life experience.' – Doctor

'This question is best argued by patients who are actually suffering and the next of kin who are on the verge of tears at the suffering of their near and dear ones.' – Doctor in A&E

'Hypocrisy is wrong in any aspect of human life and is worse when it involves the concept of human right. We are allowed to make decision on having abortion, giving birth and giving it away in the name of "surrogation" and many other issues and yet when it comes to our suffering we are told we are incapable and someone else or the society should make the decision. It is them who have the right to decide if we have had enough or not. This is not only unfair but also very undemocratic.' – Doctor

'UK should consider the issue seriously. Terminally ill patients and their relatives should have a greater say in the process and the issue should not be hijacked by pro-life campaigners.' – ITU Doctor

'Nowadays I'm aware of several cases where doctors have colluded with patients with this only to be reported by nursing/ancillary staff for their actions (but never by relatives). Doctors are no longer prepared to risk this course of action as it is stressful enough to decide to go along with their patients' requests let alone watching their backs for another party to report their actions.' – GP

'This is a really difficult area and one where I feel a real sense of dilemma where patients are clearly going to die but where I am able to control symptoms whilst their lives drag out to an inevitable and frequently difficult ending.' – GP

'We must move forward as a profession and accept a changing situation. I have been asked many times to help patients "when they are no longer fit" or dignified.' – GP

■ The above information is from ukActNow's web sitewhich can be found at www.ukActNow.org

© *ukActNow*

# No cure for medical madness

## Mercy killing and assisted suicide

*By Dr Patrick Dixon*

As a care of the dying specialist in the past I have often been asked to kill people – which is euthanasia, mercy killing or assisted suicide.

Sometimes relatives have taken me on one side and told me they cannot bear it any more: 'Isn't there something you can do to end it all?' More often requests for euthanasia have come from those who are ill. I remember visiting a man with lung cancer. He asked his wife to leave the room. As she closed the door he leaned over and grabbed my arm. 'I want to die', he said. 'Please can you give me something.' He felt a burden on his wife and wanted euthanasia for himself. People are often more afraid of the process of dying than of death itself.

The Voluntary Euthanasia Society wants to allow people 'with a severe illness from which no relief is known' to be lawfully killed if they wish. One US euthanasia campaigner has suggested people could be killed on the basis of their previous instructions, even if they now want to live. This is in the case of someone with Alzheimers disease where the person is no longer distressed about memory loss while others are.

Where do you start or stop euthanasia? How advanced must cancer be for euthanasia to be appropriate? How can you be sure? Doctors are often wrong about diagnosis or prognosis. What about other illnesses, dementia, or handicap? Who decides about euthanasia? On what basis do we judge? Are those in pain receiving proper medication? Has every appropriate treatment option been explored?

What is euthanasia? Mercy killing is the literal definition of the word euthanasia.

The hospice movement started in this country because people were dying badly, often in pain. In thirty years over 200 hospices have opened

> *Quality of life can disappear under a forest of needles, wires, electronic gadgets and needless operations*

and 240 hospitals now have specialist nurses. Almost 100,000 people each year are visited by home care teams, over half of all those dying of cancer.

Countries like Holland where euthanasia is commonly practised have poor hospice facilities. Euthanasia can be a lazy option. Doctors may never realise they have anything to learn.

Few things are more rewarding to me than visiting someone dying at home, relieving pain and other symptoms so the person can start to live again.

Restoring dignity, quality of life and giving people back control over their lives is far better than fatal injections. Most people are visibly relieved when I tell them euthanasia is not an option.

When symptoms are properly controlled, fears dealt with, practical help is provided and people feel safe, it is very rare for people to ask again for death by euthanasia.

Euthanasia will destroy trust between doctors and the dying. As it is, people commonly fear hospice care in case it shortens life. What if they find out some people are being actively killed?

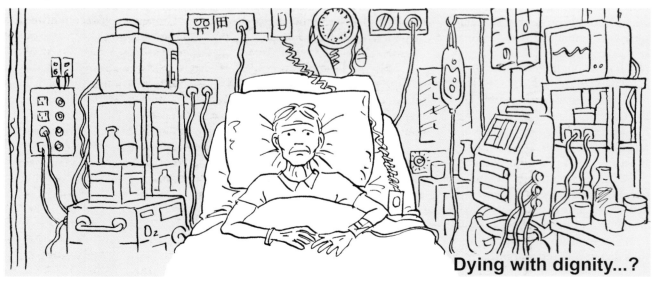

**Dying with dignity...?**

Some have said that relieving pain is a form of euthanasia anyway. This is nonsense. The strongest painkillers merely replace naturally occurring substances in the brain called endorphins, deficient in chronic or severe pain.

You don't make a junky out of someone with a broken leg just because you give an injection of heroin. The situation is quite different in someone who is healthy, well and pain free, or given a massive overdose.

I have seen people on very high levels of painkillers for long periods – there is no 'correct dose' except the dose which relieves pain. The medication has been stopped the day after special surgery or nerve blocks, with no withdrawal symptoms.

Legalised euthanasia would put at risk a generation of the elderly, frail and emotionally vulnerable as collective pressure grows to ask for early death.

Never underestimate the strains felt by the old and ill, increased with every media report of scarce resources, waiting lists and spiralling costs of high tech medicine.

Many so-called advances are merely medicine gone mad. Doctors trained to make people better are often frustrated by incurable illness. They also have to publish research to get top jobs so there is pressure to try out unproven treatments. Quality of life can disappear under a forest of needles, wires, electronic gadgets and needless operations.

Time after time I have seen those who are dying trapped in hospitals waiting for useless tests when they want to be at home. Others in coma following accidents or strokes often linger for months, hovering in that twilight zone between life and death, sustained by massive effort even when there is no hope of any meaningful future existence.

Medical madness can be horrific. A friend went into hospital at the age of 75 for surgery which found inoperable tumour. A day or two later she had a heart attack and was dying peacefully.

Despite her wishes for no heroics the 'crash' team was called and violent attempts were made to revive

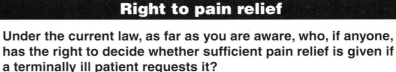

## Right to pain relief

**Under the current law, as far as you are aware, who, if anyone, has the right to decide whether sufficient pain relief is given if a terminally ill patient requests it?**

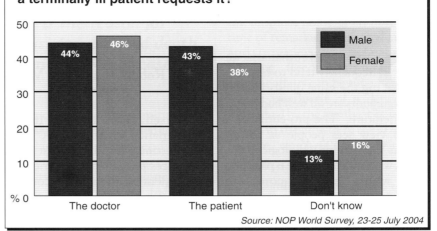

| | The doctor | The patient | Don't know |
|---|---|---|---|
| Male | 44% | 43% | 13% |
| Female | 46% | 38% | 16% |

Source: NOP World Survey, 23-25 July 2004

her with massive electric shocks and injections. She died anyway – without peace or dignity because no one stopped to think.

As a reaction many are now writing down in advance what they want to happen at the end of their lives and want it legally binding. Communication is always a good thing and anything that helps a doctor to understand a patient's wishes is surely to be encouraged. Treatment decisions are often difficult and a strongly expressed view can be very helpful – even if written in advance.

It can be hard to be allowed to die – and I am not talking about euthanasia which is a deliberate act designed to kill. If I was dying of advanced cancer with many complications I would make it clear that my next pneumonia should be my last. There is no need to 'strive officiously to keep alive', so why pump me full of antibiotics ?

However the moment such directives are backed by law then doctors will risk prosecution if the exact wording is not followed, regardless of circumstances – medicine by lawyers. But as with euthanasia, you would have to be absolutely certain the person was not depressed at the time, under pressure or feeling a burden.

How could you be sure that every medical option had been fully explained and understood, and that the diagnosis was correct? People often change their minds about

treatment when close to death. Advance directives only tell us what people felt in the past.

Involving Parliament, laws, police, magistrates, judges, jury and prisons would be an utterly disastrous way to care for the dying. New legislation is unnecessary, undesirable, inappropriate and will probably be unhelpful.

The British Medical Association agrees that Living Wills need no force of law and recently voted against euthanasia by three to one. The pro-euthanasia lobby sees legalised Living Wills as a vital next step to acceptance of euthanasia.

The real answer lies not in laws but proper medical training, good communication, compassionate common sense and expert appropriate treatment taking into account the expressed wishes of each individual.

I hope the select committee has had the courage to keep care out of court, encourage better medical training and to leave the law alone.

Editor's note: it did !

■ Dr Patrick Dixon is a former specialist in the care of those dying of cancer and AIDS. The article is based on an address given in the House of Lords recently.

■ The above information is from Global Changes' website which can be found at www.globalchange.com

© Dr Patrick Dixon

# Advance directives

## Information from the Christian Medical Fellowship

Many people are worried that serious illness may leave them 'kept alive' by medical technology. They fear that in such a state they would be unable to express their wishes about which treatments they do or do not want. Making an advance directive is one proposed solution. While these may be useful they are not without problems. It's important that everyone weighs up the strengths and limitations of such directives, as well as understands their legal status.

You are suffering from dementia and are in a nursing home. Unable to recognise your family, speak or swallow, you are fed through a tube down your nose. You have repeated chest infections and doctors keep giving you antibiotics. You would not have wanted to live like this, but the staff seem unwilling to 'let you go'.

This scenario highlights a situation that many people fear and has fuelled the debate about advance directives. Afraid of being trapped between life and death, people have sought ways of telling doctors that if they can no longer express their wishes, they would rather be allowed to die than be kept alive by extraordinary or disproportionate means. Some have chosen to record this decision in a written document termed an advance directive, or 'living will'.

In broad outline, advance directives fit in with the British Medical Association's views, which say that while 'life should be cherished despite disability and handicaps', it should not be 'indefinitely sustained in all circumstances, for example, when its prolongation by artificial means would be regarded as inhumane and the treatment itself burdensome'.[1]

While at first sight, advance directives seem to raise few ethical problems, closer examination shows they need to be treated with caution. There has also been considerable confusion about their legal status.

### By James Paul

## Background influences

Advance directives have appeared because of three key issues and influences within society.

### Call for autonomy

One powerful drive is the demand for people to make their own decisions. This call for autonomy says that, while a doctor may have a better understanding of the patient's medical needs and the likelihood of success of any particular treatment, individuals have primary responsibility for their health and must live with the consequences of any decisions. The previous paternalistic mentality of 'the doctor knows best', has been replaced with the notion of 'informed consent' – the idea that clinicians give information so that patients can make sound choices.

In reality autonomy is not that simple. In any democratic society every person has the right to personal autonomy, but other people's rights to personal autonomy necessarily restrict this. We do not tolerate a burglar's autonomous desire to rob someone else's house. Problems start when autonomy is given the status of an unbreakable principle or law.

With an advance directive, one person's desire for a particular style of treatment demands that others provide it. This may conflict with

the provider's personal and professional views of what is the best course of action. A person's refusal of treatment can also conflict with their family's desire to do everything to avoid losing a much-loved relative.

### Loss of trust

The dawn of the twenty-first century has seen a loss of trust. Many institutions and professions are under suspicion. These include the church, police, monarchy and doctors. The abuse of power shown by mass-murderer Harold Shipman, or negligence in the case of Alder Hey Hospital's unauthorised retention of organs after post-mortems, have fuelled the mistrust.

This loss of trust is not one-sided. Doctors are increasingly fearful that they will be sued if their patients don't like the outcome of any intervention; they are losing trust in their patients.

### Medical progress

Both of these are set against ever-increasing medical capability. Seldom a week goes by without some new treatment being announced. However, while these advances often sustain life, many people find that they are left with a quality of life they feel unable to bear.

There is no denying that many who would formerly have died of cardiac arrest, pneumonia or kidney failure have been given a new lease of life. On the other hand, many are left half-cured – alive but with distinct disability and declining health.

Medical progress has gone a long way to remove suffering, but now some people are pointing out that our society has lost any sense of the value that can come from adversity.

At the same time, medical progress has caused a further problem. While it has enabled more people to live to old age, many of these have conditions like Alzheimer's disease. Consequently some people now fear degradation and indignity from degenerative diseases far more than death itself.

### Arguments for . . .

There is a clear call to help people express their autonomy, protect themselves from what some see as a self-serving medical profession, and avoid any potentially damaging effects of medical technology.

People argue that advance directives can help them to:

- avoid degrading and drawn-out treatment for a terminal illness
- achieve a death with dignity, or a 'good death' (although this is often not defined very well)
- avoid the expense of medical costs during a prolonged final illness
- avoid breaching a patient's personal or religious beliefs

In addition, some doctors believe that advance directives will give them some protection in the event of a patient's death or disability. In effect, they hope that the directive removes some of their responsibility.

### Arguments against . . .

There is, however, a number of reasons why the situation is not that straight forward.

#### Uncertain outcome

Advance directives often state that 'in the event of "x" medical condition occurring with no chance of recovery, I would want "y" to be done'. In order for a doctor to carry out this directive he has to be certain of several things. First that he is certain in his diagnosis that the patient has medical condition 'x'. Secondly that there is no chance of recovery if given suitable treatment.

---

*A study of 21 people who were paralysed from the neck down and needed ventilators to help them breathe, found that only one person wished that she had been allowed to die*

---

This is seldom easy to do and people are known to make remarkable and unexpected recoveries. It can be particularly difficult to predict the outcome of emergency treatment.

Predicting an outcome presupposes that you have correctly diagnosed the illness or disease. If you don't know what is wrong, it is going to be very difficult to come up with any meaningful predictions of outcome. One study showed that about half of the cases of Persistent Vegetative State are incorrectly diagnosed.[2] Requiring two or more doctors to agree on a prognosis simply reduces the error, but does little to eliminate the problem.

#### New attitudes

Trying to imagine what it would be like to be terminally ill is one thing. Being terminally ill is quite another and people's attitudes and wishes frequently change with the onset of serious illness. It appears that life often seems more precious when it is more precarious, and most patients when confronted with a choice between death and seriously disabled life, choose life.

A study of 21 people who were paralysed from the neck down and needed ventilators to help them breathe, found that only one person wished that she had been allowed to die. Two were undecided, but the remaining 18 were pleased to be alive.[3] It is reasonable to believe that while healthy, they would have said they would rather die than live in this highly-dependent state.

#### New treatments

When writing an advance directive, a person will make assumptions based on current abilities of technology to control pain or other symptoms. Developments in medical practice are increasing our ability to make life comfortable, and the advance directive may not be able to take these changes into account.

#### New circumstances

Many events in life can influence one's attitude to disability. For example, the arrival of a grandchild can give an elderly person a new reason for wanting to continue living, and changes in religious conviction can revolutionise a person's attitudes to life, death and disability. Even without religious convictions, many people come to see real meaning and purpose in their suffering.

Doctors need to do everything possible to check that a patient hasn't changed his or her mind, rather than simply relying on an advance directive. A study of 150 competent people with advance directives concluded that 61% thought there could be times when their best interests would be served if clinicians ignored their directive.[4]

- Euthanasia originally meant 'a gentle and easy death', and is now used to mean 'the act of inducing an easy death', usually referring to acts which terminate or shorten life painlessly in order to end suffering where there is no prospect of recovery. (p. 1)

- Some religious people maintain that there is a moral distinction between acts which cause death (active euthanasia) and omissions which cause death (passive euthanasia), only the second being morally permissible. (p. 2)

- Oregon, the Netherlands and Belgium are the only jurisdictions in the world where laws specifically permit euthanasia or assisted suicide. Oregon permits assisted suicide. The Netherlands and Belgium permit both euthanasia and assisted suicide. (page 3)

- Euthanasia and assisted suicide are not private acts. Rather, they involve one person facilitating the death of another. This is a matter of very public concern since it can lead to tremendous abuse, exploitation and erosion of care for the most vulnerable people among us. (p. 4)

- In 1996, 54 per cent of 1,000 doctors questioned in a survey said they were in favour of legalising physician-assisted suicide in specific circumstances. The same survey found 3 per cent of GPs had helped terminally ill patients to die. (p. 9)

- It was revealed in September 2004, that 50% of Britons would be prepared to go abroad to seek medical help to die if they were terminally ill. (p. 10)

- Anyone helping another person to commit suicide can now be prosecuted under UK law, though a ban on anyone attempting suicide was scrapped in 1961. (p. 11)

- The term passive euthanasia is used by some people to describe situations where a doctor deliberately allows a person to die. Some bioethicists say that in these situations 'killing' is the same as 'letting die'. But the term 'passive euthanasia' is confusing. (p. 12)

- In England and Wales a person who assists in the suicide of another or an attempted suicide is liable to imprisonment for up to 14 years. (p. 15)

- In the UK we do not know how many deaths are as a result of assisted dying. We do not know how many non-voluntary assisted dying cases there are, although the evidence suggests that it may be as high as 18,000 per year. (p. 16)

- Opinion polls show overwhelming public support for law changes that would make it easier for terminally ill patients in pain to request medical help to shorten their lives. (p. 17)

- Unlike Italy, Switzerland, Denmark, Belgium, Sweden, Norway, the Netherlands and Australia, the British Government has never, and refuses to, commission research into the frequency of assisted dying in the United Kingdom. (p. 20)

- Physician-assisted suicide (PAS) generally refers to a practice in which the physician provides a patient with a lethal dose of medication, upon the patient's request, which the patient intends to use to end his or her own life. (p. 22)

- A recent *Nursing Times* survey (Hemmings 2003) found that two out of three nurses thought there should be legislation for assisted dying; one in four had been asked by a patient to help them end their life. (p. 27)

- When symptoms are properly controlled, fears dealt with, practical help is provided and people feel safe, it is very rare for people to ask again for death by euthanasia. (p. 28)

- The new mental capacity bill, introduced in parliament in June 2004, has been designed to protect people who lack capacity or have fluctuating capacity to express, in advance, a decision to refuse medical treatment provided by health professionals. (p. 32)

- A living will can take various forms, but usually it is a written document setting out the circumstances under which you would not want to receive life-prolonging medical treatment. (p. 33)

- Living wills should be reviewed regularly, as it is important that you have not changed your mind between the date of making the living will and the date when you fall mentally incompetent. (p. 34)

- There is a clear call to help people express their autonomy, protect themselves from what some see as a self-serving medical profession, and avoid any potentially damaging effects of medical technology. (p. 37)

- People also argue that advance directives are virtually useless in practice. This is because the exact situations described in an advance directive hardly ever arise. The effect is that clinicians still have to decide what is in the patient's best interests. (p. 38)

You might like to contact the following organisations for further information. Due to the increasing cost of postage, many organisations cannot respond to enquiries unless they receive a stamped, addressed envelope.

## ALERT
27 Walpole Street
London, SW3 4QS
Tel: 020 7730 2800
Fax: 020 7730 1710
E-mail: alert@donoharm.org.uk
Website: www.donoharm.org.uk/alert
The aim of ALERT is to warn people of the dangers of any type of euthanasia legislation and pro-death initiatives. These include the promotion of Living Wills and Advance Directives, which create a climate for the acceptance of euthanasia.

## British Humanist Association (BHA)
1 Gower Street
London, WC1E 6HD
Tel: 020 7079 3580
Fax: 020 7079 3588
E-mail: info@humanism.org.uk
Website: www.humanism.org.uk
The British Humanist Association is the UK's leading organisation for people concerned with ethics and society, free from religious and supernatural dogma. It represents, supports and serves humanists in the United Kingdom and is a registered charity with more than fifty affiliated local groups. Publishes a wide range of free briefings including the issues of racism, discrimination and prejudice, abortion, euthanasia and surrogacy.

## Canadian Physicians for Life
10150 Gillanders Road
Chilliwack
BC V2P 6H4, Canada
Tel: + 1 604 794 3772
Fax: + 1 604 794 3960
E-mail: info@physiciansforlife.ca
Website: www.physiciansforlife.ca
Founded in 1975, Canadian Physicians for Life are a non-profit, charitable organisation of Canadian physicians dedicated to the respect and ethical treatment of every human being, regardless of age or infirmity.

## Christian Medical Fellowship (CMF)
Partnership House
157 Waterloo Road
London, SE1 8XN
Tel: 020 7928 4694
Fax: 020 7620 2453
E-mail: admin@cmf.org.uk
Website: www.cmf.org.uk
A network of approximately 4,500 doctors and 600 medical students throughout the UK and Republic of Ireland which opposes euthanasia. They produce a range of booklets and leaflets, including CMF files.

## International Task Force on Euthanasia and Assisted Suicide
PO Box 760
Steubenville, OH 43952
USA
Tel: + 1 740 282 3810
Fax: + 1 740 282 0769
Website: www.internationaltaskforce.org
The International Anti-Euthanasia Task Force (IAETF) is an international leader in the ever-increasing debate over assisted suicide and euthanasia. The IAETF concentrates solely on the issues surrounding assisted suicide and euthanasia and addresses these issues from a public policy perspective.

## Making Decisions Alliance
c/o Mental Health Foundation/Foundation for People with Learning Disabilities
Sea Containers House
20 Upper Ground
London, SE1 9QB
Tel: 020 7802 0300
Fax: 020 7802 0313
Website: www.makingdecisions.org.uk
The Making Decisions Alliance (MDA) was formed because the current legal situation with mental incapacity is totally inadequate and affects so many people.

## The Patients Association
PO Box 935
Harrow
Middlesex, HA1 3YJ
Tel: 020 8423 9111
Fax: 020 8423 9119
E-mail: mailbox@patients-association.com
Website: www.patients-association.com
For help and information please call our Helpline between 10.00am and 4.00pm Mondays-Fridays 0845 6084455.

## ProLife Party
PO Box 13395
London, SW3 6XE
Tel: 020 7581 6939
Fax: 020 7581 3868
E-mail: info@prolife.org.uk
Website: www.prolife.org.uk
The ProLife Party is Europe's first Pro-Life Political Party.

## UKActNow.org
13 Prince of Wales Terrace
London, W8 5PG
Tel: 020 7937 7781
E-mail: campaign@ukactnow.org
Website: www.UKActNow.org
The ukActNow team came together after Diane Pretty, who had the terminal illness Motor Neurone Disease, lost her legal battle for the right to choose medical assistance to die with dignity and avoid what she considered to be a distressing death and unnecessary suffering.

## Voluntary Euthanasia Society
13 Prince of Wales Terrace
London, W8 5PG
Tel: 020 7937 7770
Fax: 020 7376 2648
E-mail: info@ves.org.uk
Website: www.ves.org.uk
The Voluntary Euthanasia Society (UK) campaigns for wider choice at the end of life. As well as our political campaign to legalise assisted dying, we also supply living will forms for the advance refusal of medical treatment.

# INDEX

# ACKNOWLEDGEMENTS

The publisher is grateful for permission to reproduce the following material.

While every care has been taken to trace and acknowledge copyright, the publisher tenders its apology for any accidental infringement or where copyright has proved untraceable. The publisher would be pleased to come to a suitable arrangement in any such case with the rightful owner.

### Chapter One: The Moral Debate

A non-religious perspective on euthanasia, © British Humanist Association, So you think you know about euthanasia?, © Alert, Euthanasia and assisted suicide, © 2005 International Task Force on Euthanasia and Suicide, The law and euthanasia, © NOP World Survey, Assisting the terminally ill, © Guardian Newspapers Limited 2004, 'I don't want to plan my death, I want to enjoy life', © Guardian Newspapers Limited 2004, ProLife Party responds to poll, © ProLife Party, Support for change of the law, © 2004 Voluntary Euthanasia Society (UK), The results, © NOP World Survey, Disabled people want the right to die, © Guardian Newspapers Limited 2004, Euthanasia, © Christian Medical Fellowship, The law is not working, © 2004 Voluntary Euthanasia Society (UK), Trust, © YouGov, Going abroad, © NOP World Survey.

### Chapter Two: The Medical Debate

Revealed: full scale of euthanasia in Britain, © Guardian Newspapers Limited 2004, The future of the right-to-die movement, © Derek Humphry 2004, Medically assisted dying in the UK, © 2004 Voluntary Euthanasia Society (UK), Nurses support a change in the law, © 2004 Voluntary Euthanasia Society (UK), Assisted suicide, © The World Federation of Right to Die Societies, Pain relief, © NOP World Survey, Swiss charity says its clients 'die with dignity', © Telegraph Group Limited, London 2004, Secret killings of newborn babies, © Guardian Newspapers Limited 2004, Professionals speak, © ukActNow, No cure for medical madness, © Dr Patrick Dixon, Right to pain relief, © NOP World Survey, Refuting the rhetoric, © Canadian Physicians for Life 1998-2005.

### Chapter Three: Living Wills

Thinking ahead, © Guardian Newspapers Limited 2004, Assistance to die, © NOP World Survey, Living wills, © The Patients Association, A matter of birth and death, © laterlife.com, Advance directives, © Christian Medical Fellowship, Living wills, © Making Decisions Alliance, Chaos as 'living will' law passed, © Telegraph Group Limited, London 2005.

### Photographs and illustrations:

Pages 1, 26, 37: Simon Kneebone; pages 8, 33: Bev Aisbett; pages 12, 28: Angelo Madrid; pages 19, 25: Pumpkin House; pages 20, 34: Don Hatcher.

Craig Donnellan
Cambridge
April, 2005